HOW TO **SAVE** YOUR **DAUGHTER'S LIFE**

HOW TO **SAVE** YOUR
DAUGHTER'S
LIFE

Straight Talk for Parents from
America's Top Criminal Profiler

PAT BROWN

Health Communications, Inc.
Deerfield Beach, Florida

www.hcibooks.com

Library of Congress Cataloging-in-Publication Data

Brown, Pat.
    How to save your daughter's life : straight talk for parents from America's top criminal profiler / Pat Brown.
        p. cm.
    ISBN 13: 978-0-7573-1669-2 (trade paper)
    ISBN 10: 0-7573-1669-7 (trade paper)
    ISBN 13: 978-0-7573-1670-8 (e-pub)
    ISBN 10: 0-7573-1670-0 (e-pub)
    1. Young women—Sexual behavior.   2. Daughters—Sexual behavior.
    3. Sex crimes—Prevention.   4. Women—Crimes against—Prevention.
    I. Title.
    HQ27.5.B76 2012
    306.7084'22--dc23
    2012017982

Publisher: Health Communications, Inc.
            3201 S.W. 15th Street
            Deerfield Beach, FL 33442–8190

Cover design by Dane Wesolko
Interior design and formatting by Lawna Patterson Oldfield

Contents

● ●

Introduction: Important! Read First!   vii

One: **The Early Years** 1

Two: **Partying, Drinking, Drugging, Casual Sex (Hooking Up), and Gangs** 39

Three: **Date Rape** 65

Four: **The Dangers of Social Networking and the Internet** 89

Five: **Risky Relationships** 129

Six: **Stalkers** 169

Seven: **Child Predators, Serial Rapists, and Serial Killers** 193

Eight: **The Sex Trade and Sex Trafficking** 221

Final Thoughts 245

About the Author 247

Index 249

Introduction:
Important! Read First!

Whenever young women meet tragic ends—a jogger who is raped and murdered by a serial killer, a teenager who is killed by her boyfriend after she breaks up with him, a high school girl who gets beat up by a group of girls she thought were her friends, or a series of prostitutes go missing after advertising on Craigslist—my phone starts ringing. I spend the next few days on *The Today Show*, *The Early Show*, *Nancy Grace*, *Jane Velez-Mitchell*, *Inside Edition*, *FOX and Friends*, *Dr. Drew*, or HLN's *Prime News* talking about what kind of person would commit such a horrendous crime. I often discuss how the poor woman or girl ended up a victim and give advice to other females on how to avoid a similar situation. I hope to save lives by sharing some thoughts that maybe haven't occurred to some of the viewers or that might remind them of certain behaviors or choices that can put them in harm's way.

Usually after the shows, I get e-mails from many people thanking me for sharing information that can keep them or their loved ones from harm. Here are two e-mails I received following my July 2011 appearance on *The Today Show* when I spoke of the brutal murder of high school graduate Lauren Astley by her ex-boyfriend:

Ms. Brown:

I just saw you on The Today Show *speaking about a recent tragedy involving the violent murder of a recent high school graduate by, police believe, her boyfriend.*

In that interview you spoke directly to girls who have recently broken up with their partner, advising that if that partner requests a meeting post-breakup that it not be done privately because the partner is counting on the fact that she's nice and will agree to meet.

I can't agree with you enough!

I fear however that we—in particular women—don't actually teach our girls that it's okay to refuse that "one last time" or that it's Okay and likely wise to break up in a public place or over the phone even, when one's partner exhibits dangerous traits.

Moreover, we don't even do a good job of teaching our girls how, in the depths of teenage love, to spot the subtle signs that scream "danger." Nor do we teach them how to put words to those gut instincts that tell us something is amiss with our partner and relationship, or, simply, that we deserve better than what we've been experiencing in the relationship at hand. We do, however, do a great job of teaching them that it's important to be nice, understanding, caring, and nurturing without also teaching them to be wise and deeply instinctual, as though the former and latter attributes are mutually exclusive.

So thank you for your very frank statement. It is my sincere hope, however, that you are able to carry that statement widely to girls and women everywhere as I truly believe we are needlessly losing our sisters to the false idea that our gender requires us to be "nice" and "nurturing" in all circumstances.

Best regards, Aurora Vasquez

Dear Ms. Brown,

Thank you for being the only voice [I hear] in the media calling domestic and dating violence what it is: power and control. Anchors and interviewers insist on trying to spin the "he just snapped" angle . . . "he was a great kid, great guy, wonderful man . . . what caused him to snap all of a sudden?"

You made that point this morning on The Today Show, countering the therapist's comments and speaking directly to girls and women. Giving them information that could save their lives.

THANK YOU, THANK YOU, THANK YOU . . .

Sincerely, Tina Tucker
Lincoln County Community Educator, New Hope for
Women, P.O. Box A, Rockland, ME 04841-0733

And then I get hate mail from angry people claiming I am blaming the victim. They think I am saying it is the woman's fault for what happened. They truly feel I am implying the victim deserved what she got and that I am taking away the responsibility from the perpetrator. They write that the victim is not at fault in any way, no matter what she did or where she chose to go or with whom she had a relationship at the time.

Well, I agree that the perpetrator is entirely to blame for committing the crime. Violent crime is illegal, inhumane, and immoral. And it is true no one deserves to be murdered, even if she was out selling her body on the street or was buying drugs in a bad part of town or was cheating on her boyfriend with his brother. But there *are* behaviors victims engage in that may bring them into harm's way, and it's terribly important to be honest about this; how else can we save women's lives, especially our daughters' lives, if we refuse to recognize or admit that there are things they might do that will get them raped or murdered? Young people need to hear the message loud and clear—and so do their parents. After years on the front lines profiling criminals, I know that parents and their daughters need specific facts about how one becomes a victim, and they need guidance to help avoid such a fate.

To put it bluntly, talking about the perpetrator may be fascinating and educational, and we can rail about changing the system, locking these monsters up, and preventing them from being created in the first place, but it isn't going to do much to save your daughter's life today. It is like this: Suppose a young girl goes out on the African plain alone for a walk in nature. She gets eaten by a lion. Should I speak about how bad the lion is? How he shouldn't have eaten the girl? Should I go talk to that lion and the other lions and tell them not to eat people? Are those lions going to pay me any mind?

Murderous psychopaths, like lions, don't care what I have to say. I can't stop them or teach them to do right. I can't stop a lion. I can't stop an inhumane human. Unless I can lock them all up right now (that is, if I even knew which ones were lions or about to become lions), some girl, somewhere, is at risk. That girl might be your daughter. I can't make quick changes to get rid of all psychopaths and predators out there, but I can educate mothers and fathers on lion behavior and lion territory and help them help their daughters avoid these beasts and defend themselves, if they must.

In this book, I hope to help you understand the world of psychopaths and criminals: how they think, where they lurk, and how they lure and grab victims. Then you can make your daughter's world safer and teach her how to avoid those exact situations in which she might end up being harmed by a psychopath or someone who does not have her well-being as his or her concern. I will discuss what kinds of choices and defenses will protect her and which ones are dangerous. Each chapter in this book also has suggestions for the more willful child, and at the end of the chapter is a "Letter to My Daughter" that even a defiant daughter may benefit from.

I urge you as you read this book to recognize that I am not trying to insult you or your daughter in any way by talking about parenting decisions and teenage behaviors. We do the best we can with what we know, and kids will be kids and that is why they need parents. The fact that you are reading this book shows me you care about your daughter and you know it is a rather scary world we live in. Let's make it safer for her.

WARNING: *I speak in a very open fashion about sex, violence, relationships, prostitution, drugs, alcohol, rape, murder, crime, criminals, and psychopaths. I do not beat around the bush and couch what I say in soothing words or in psychobabble. I may take on the thinking of the predator or psychopath and show you what he might be planning for your daughter, and it isn't particularly sweet. I hope you understand I simply want to be clear and straightforward, with no BS. Better a bit of discomfort here than massive heartache later.*

· ·

One

THE **EARLY** YEARS

*K**eeping your daughter safe* starts when she is little. Providing a loving home, a supportive community, a good schooling situation, interesting hobbies, inspiring goals, and discipline early on lays a strong foundation for your teenager to make good choices, respect your decisions, and come to you for advice. Understanding the negative impact of certain video games, literature, television, and films is important to channel your daughter's interests and behaviors in a healthy direction.

There is an old joke that when one's baby is born, the parents cry and thank God for blessing them with such a wonderful gift. Then when the child becomes a teen, the parents ask God what they did wrong to deserve such punishment! All joking aside, there is a deeply embedded belief that all teenagers are a nightmare; that they will rebel, get in various sorts of trouble, and will hate their parents, at least on and off. I have to wonder if we are not fulfilling our expectations. I remember being rather perplexed when my friends with children a few years older than mine would knowingly warn me, "Just wait until she's two!" (she will have temper tantrums), "Just wait until she's twelve!" (she will start being defiant), "Just wait until she's sixteen!" (she will be sneaky and disobedient). Why do they all assume children have to act badly in each of these stages?

I did note that a number of these negative behaviors were indeed evident in many neighborhood children. I saw two-year-olds rolling around on the ground kicking and screaming, young boys throwing their bats or helmets on the baseball field when they struck out, and teenage girls screaming, "You're stupid!" at their moms and dads. Thankfully, not all children acted this way and not all children acted this way consistently, but clearly there were children whom parents were having problems disciplining and getting respect from. My three children were not perfect children, but I never had much problem with their behavior, at home or in pubic, and none of them ever cursed at me or told me they hated me (they may have muttered it, but they didn't voice it loud enough for me to hear).

So what is the point I am making here? If you lose control of your children in their early years, it is hard to get them to obey you or take your advice when they become teenagers. Some parents who give in too much (because they get tired of being tough or they want their kids to like them) find their children rule them and run wild when they get older and have more freedom. And then it's nearly impossible to tame that wild horse you've got who is always trying to run away from the stable and break free of your control. If your daughter is still very young at the time you read this book, keep this in mind: you are sowing now what you will reap later. Better to be tough when they are little and then slowly let out the reins than be too easy when they are small and create a monster for a teen. If your daughter is already a handful, you just have to do your best to guide her within the situation you find yourself.

Let me suggest a few important things to do as your children are growing up. One is to not allow your child to be abusive toward adults and other children; tantrums, biting, hitting, spiteful words, and blatant disobedience are not acceptable behavior. Not only does behaving badly harm others, such behavior harms the child as well and allows her to be self-ish, narcissistic, nonempathetic human beings. Such behaviors should be immediately brought to a halt by removing the child from the environment, sternly reprimanding her for her meanness, and implementing some punishment or discipline. It may be really hard work, but believe me, you will have so much less work when she is older; you won't be babysitting your grandchild while your daughter goes to high school, you won't be hiding your jewelry from your crack-addicted young adult child, and you will not be visiting her at the jail where she is incarcerated for her fifth crime.

How to Control, Not Cave, in a Nice Way

By the way, punishment isn't about being physical—spanking, slapping, or beating up your child. Punishment and discipline should be educational and teach a lesson (and that lesson isn't "Your parent is a thug."). Is it fair to not tell your child what behavior is expected and then punish her for something she didn't know was wrong? The best time to explain what behaviors your children should exhibit is prior to entering any situation. You need to explain yourself clearly and make sure they understand (they should repeat back to you the expected behavior). This education needs to be repeated until doing so makes your children roll their eyes and say, "We *know*, Mom!"

Let me share a few examples of how I used this method with my children when they were fairly young.

When my children and I first started making our weekly trips to the library, I would stop before we went inside and tell them how they were to behave. "Okay, kids, we are going into the library, which is a place where we are to be very quiet. It is not a playground; we don't run around and make noise in there. People are reading and studying, so we are to move quietly and whisper so they are not disturbed. Okay?" Then I would take them in and make sure they were following the rules. Afterward, I would praise them. If they veered, I would immediately take action. If they started to move too fast, I would put a restraining hand on them. I'd do the same if they raised their voices. It really only took a few times before they had the proper behavior down and I didn't have to mention it again.

When I took my two sons to the baseball field for their games, I gave them a very stern warning in the beginning. I told them in no uncertain terms that good sportsmanship was expected. I explained this meant no talking back to the coach, no throwing of the bat or helmet when they struck out, and no spitting in their palms before they shook hands with the winning team. I told them that while I understood their desire to be chosen to be on the field, to get home runs, and to win the game, it was still a game, and if a game was going to cause them to treat others badly or to act like brats, they didn't need to play. Partway through the season a couple of parents asked me why my sons never acted out on the field, and I told them, "Because they aren't allowed to."

Here is a really proud moment I had with my children when my daughter was seven and my boys were five. We had accompanied my husband out of town for the day, and while he was working, we went to a restaurant in town to eat. After we entered the restaurant, I realized that it was pretty fancy and here I was with three little urchins, not all that well dressed. My children were hungry and it was the only restaurant I had seen, so I decided we would go ahead and eat there. As the waiter led us to our table, I saw a couple in their sixties looking horrified as we took our seats.

I whispered to my kids, "Do you see that man and lady at the next table? Do you see how worried they look? They are like Grandma and Grandpa, and I bet they came to this restaurant to have a lovely lunch and they are thinking that you kids are going to be loud and obnoxious and ruin their special time together. So let's surprise them and make sure they have a wonderful lunch. Let's only whisper while we eat and work really hard to make sure our utensils don't make clanging noises on the plate." And the kids did exactly that. It was actually pretty funny to watch them being so careful while they ate. It was all worth it when the couple came over to our table and said, "We just want to tell you we were very worried when you and your children came in, but your children are so well behaved, we are just amazed! We want to thank your children for making our lunch so nice." This incident was one that showed my children how their good behavior could make people happy and that gave them pride in themselves.

As I said, my kids weren't perfect children growing up, and

I wasn't the perfect mother (I had moments when I lost it and screamed in frustration like a banshee). My adult children still joke that one of my disciplining methods—to lecture them for a lo-o-o-o-ong time (obviously done enough for them to know to pull up chairs when I began my talk)—was true torture. They laugh now and say they would have preferred me to hit them. Hey, they hated my lectures, but it kept me from physically disciplining them, they got some points from my extended talk, and I was able to let my frustration out in a safe manner. Best of all, they lived in fear of the next lecture, so they didn't want to tick me off enough to get one.

You aren't a perfect parent, either. By the time your children are grown, I am sure they will have stories to tell *their* children that you wish you could erase. But putting out the effort to be a good parent, a responsible parent, will pay off in the long run. Every parent will have slightly different techniques according to his or her background, culture, and personality, but raising children with an even mix of love and discipline usually brings good results. If you have rather fallen down in this department and are struggling, pick yourself up off the mat and work to find methods to help your children in the best way you can.

"Because I Said So" Is Lame

Although children may do dumb things, they aren't imbeciles. Even at a young age, they can understand logic to a good degree and respond well to things that make sense. My grandmother once told me I couldn't go to a football game because I might fall down the bleachers! I was sixteen years old. I looked at her like she was senile. I am sure she actually had a more logical reason for refusing me permission to go that evening, but instead of telling me the truth, she came up with an excuse I did not buy. With logic you can explain why you are saying no to your child or why she must or must not do something. You can explain in a way that will allow her to agree with (or at least understand) your reasoning. This helps her to respect you as a parent and also teaches her something about why good behavior or certain choices are better. "Because I told you so!" may show who is in authority but is a rather asinine statement—and your child knows it.

"Why can't I go to Megan's house?" your daughter demands to know when you won't permit her to visit her friend after school. "Because I said so!" tells her nothing and makes her think you are just being stupid, selfish, or mean. "Because Megan's mom has a drinking problem and she has a creepy boyfriend hanging around" is much more sensible. You can further explain why these things are concerning to you. Then help make an alternative plan like having Megan come to your house. If her mom is an alcoholic and hangs out with some loser dude, she probably won't mind getting rid of Megan for a while.

My sons once wanted to go with their baseball coach to an out-of-state Babe Ruth tournament. The coach was going to have the boys on the team share a few motel rooms near the field. My husband and I said no. My boys thought it would be lots of fun and were bummed they would be left out of the group experience. They whined and asked why they couldn't go. I explained that the coach worried me. He was a single man of about thirty who acted very immature and seemed to be too chummy with the boys, especially the smaller, slim, docile boys. Actually, he didn't seem to like my two boys that much; they were bigger and bolder, and he often appeared annoyed with them. But I told them I didn't trust him because he seemed like he could possibly be a pedophile and I didn't want to take the chance. I asked them how they would feel if they woke up in the night in that motel to find their coach lying next to them. They made faces and said, "Creepy!" and seemed to get the picture. I made alternative arrangements for the trip. My husband took off work and we drove up together and got our own motel room. Everything went fine, everyone had a good time, and nothing bad seemed to have happened.

One morning about two years later, my sons came banging on my bedroom door, whooping and shouting, "Mom! Mom! You're not gonna believe this!" They shoved the local paper under my nose and pointed to one of the news stories. "Local Catholic School Teacher (aka my boy's ex–baseball coach) Arrested for Child Sexual Assault." Seems their coach was bringing boys home from the school and offering them liquor and porn movies and sexually molesting them. Horrifying thing to happen to those young boys, but was I ever relieved I never let my sons alone with the man. And I gained credibility in my sons' eyes for profiling that right and keeping them from harm.

Slow Her Down

It is also wise not to allow freedom too quickly. Once you let the genie out of the bottle, you can't put it back in. Think about sex. Remember back to a first kiss. That first kiss usually takes a while; one first flirts, then dodges, then gets closer and closer and then, finally, allows it. The next time there is less coyness. After a while, it isn't a big deal to kiss, so sometimes a girl barely gets into the car before the guy is slobbering all over her and she is allowing it. Then comes further exploration. Unless she is waiting until marriage for sex, this eventually happens while dating. Now, moms and dads, how many of you who had sex before marriage in a long-term relationship and then broke up (or even just had sex with a one-night stand) went back to just kissing and didn't have sex again until you got married? Not too many, I would bet. Been there, done that, did it again without thinking too much about it.

And so it goes with everything. Most behaviors continue and even escalate unless one has a really bad experience. We move on and forward, not backward, in most cases. The younger one starts messing with anything, the sooner one goes to the next level. If you allow dating at age twelve, your daughter has six more years of dating before she reaches adulthood. What are the chances she will have sex in those years—and have sex earlier than a girl who doesn't start dating until age seventeen? What are the chances she will have a teenage pregnancy because she has more sexual encounters at a younger and dumber age? Think about it this way: If your daughter gets her driver's license as soon as she is legally allowed and is given a car to drive, what are the chances she will crash into a tree while taking a corner too fast or texting while driving? Won't her odds be worse than if she waits a bit longer to get her license and has to drive for a year with a parent riding shotgun before she has the opportunity to drive her own vehicle? Every year and month you can delay improves your chances of having her maturity increase enough to handle these more adult responsibilities and choices.

Also, the slower she gains these opportunities, the less she expects to be given free rein and the more she accepts her parents having a say over her activities. If you require your daughter to prove a certain maturity level before embarking on independent forays, then you can have more confidence that she will fare well in them. She will also learn that to get more freedom, she has to show she can handle it. If this is a continuous methodology you have established with her, there will be less friction and more pride as she achieves each level. Allowing her to be a part of winning such freedoms also allows her to feel she has some control over her life rather than feeling her parents are keeping her locked down or she is breaking the rules to get what she wants. She can learn to work with her parents' concerns and have good experiences doing it.

My daughter was homeschooled until she graduated from high school. Because of this, she had a wonderful and safe group of friends in her life from the homeschool group and the churches we attended. Because I had a lot of trusted adult friends in these groups, she had opportunities to spend time at others' homes and socialize in secure environments. During her high school years she wanted to join the Girl Scouts, and it was a wonderful experience. Her leader was very energetic and involved the girls in lots of fabulous activities and local trips to historic sites and cultural events. Some of the girls came from, well, screwed-up families, and they were a bit more wild than the homeschoolers or church mates. While I didn't allow her to hang out with them outside of the Girl Scout activities, she had fun with them in group situations with an adult present. This was a step I allowed for her to be with some girls of different backgrounds as she matured, and I felt she had a strong enough upbringing to understand different kinds of people without getting off track or having too much freedom to overexplore.

I didn't allow dating until she was eighteen, but I allowed her to "like a boy" within group situations. She planned a wonderful sweet-sixteen party at home and invited her "boyfriend" and her teen friends and their families. We had a Roaring Twenties party complete with flapper costumes for the girls and suits and hats of the era for the boys. We had a "speakeasy" and "gambling" and jazz music. She danced her first teen dance with her dad and then with her guy. We took black-and-white photos, and we have fantastic memories of that party.

Fast forward. She grew up, joined the fire department, became a police officer, then became a child-abuse detective. She's a great adult and I am proud of her. I won't say she has never been naughty, but she controls the streets now, she doesn't work them! Whew! I recognize that some parents who have strong religious beliefs might think I should have been stricter and some more liberal folks probably think I should have been more lenient. We all have our own beliefs, and I am not trying to tell you that what I did is what you should do. I'm just saying that you need to think about how you can help your daughter make it to adulthood without getting there too soon.

I want to discuss a far too common belief in our world today: that it is normal for teens to have early sexual experiences, dark thoughts, depression, anger, and antisocial behaviors; that these behaviors are a phase that our kids will grow out of. I disagree with the idea it is natural for teens to act out. Negative thoughts and behaviors often continue into adulthood and can have life-long consequences, and they may even erupt into homicidal or suicidal behavior. Teens should *not* be unhappy people. Barring rare medical conditions, it is *not* normal for young people to be miserable, hateful, and constantly in despair. Teens may be excit-able, irrational, hormonal, and a bit emotional, but they should be positive, enthusiastic, and hopeful. Children learn from their environments, and we are failing dismally in our modern culture to provide nice places for our children to grow up in. We are allowing extremely negative and highly damaging influences into our children's world, because we don't recognize the impact these things have on our children—or we simply don't care (sometimes because we enjoy these things ourselves). Worse, some parents even introduce violent and perverse ideation into their children's lives to harden them in preparation for adulthood, believing they need to get a taste of "reality"in order to handle the real world later on. Garbage. My children grew up in a pretty nice world, and they have perfectly fine social and coping skills; they have traveled all over the world, lived in countries that are struggling with extreme poverty, and worked in law enforcement and have successfully navigated each of these environments. They are not naïve, nor are they Pollyannas or wimps. In fact, their protected upbringing made them strong and secure; they know who they are and they know what kind of people they want to be.

I am not talking here about children growing up in unfortunate situations. If you live in a war zone, in an inner-city gang area, or in serious poverty, then your children have to be helped to overcome their circumstances, be strong in spite of those issues, and see goodness and hope beyond them. But many children are growing up in relative comfort, in homes with a mass of electronics and toys, with good educations and even two parents who are gainfully employed, yet they are miserable teens, hateful, and mean. Why? What causes them to be so unappreciative of such fortune? In a nutshell, parents have allowed negativity of all sorts to poison their children's minds. Just as we can't feed our children lots of junk food and then wonder why they are ill and obese, we can't fill our children's world with unhealthy inputs and expect them to be psychologically healthy and happy.

Our home environments should be places of safety, comfort, and positive learning experiences. Yet families are disintegrating, and single parents are struggling to raise their children with consistent values while those children are shuttled between two homes with different sets of rules and incoming and outgoing "family" members. Even solid, two-parent homes often struggle with extended day care or leaving children unattended because both parents work long hours. Moms and dads are overworked and overtired, often with little help to deal with the stresses of life and raising children.

We all know these lifestyles are not the best for children, but sometimes we find ourselves in them and we must keep going. We tend to recognize that parents away at work too much isn't the best home environment for our kids. What we fail to recognize is that whether we have the perfect family situation or one with more challenges, we can control many other factors; we don't need to allow the other kinds of poison we bring into our children's world with little thought. This is something much easier for us to fix than broken homes.

Who Let the Dogs In?

What are these poisons? Television, movies, videos, music, video games, computers, books, and the Internet. These are inputs that are taking over our children's lives and minds. Think back one hundred years. What did families have to monitor? Yes, books. That is it. Books. Maybe a wandering sideshow or circus, but those were things you took your children to; they weren't sitting around your house making trouble. And if you did bring something home like a book, it didn't multiply behind your back like websites on a computer.

But regardless of the fact that everyone has these modern technologies, you have the choice to allow them in your house (or not), and you choose how they will be accessed and used. You are the adults who own the house and pay for everything in it; you are the gatekeepers, and you get to decide what comes over the moat into your castle.

Before I discuss what is detrimental about much of what children are receiving into their brains, I want to stomp the often used defense that this stuff doesn't have all that much influence on our kids. Think about this: How much does an advertiser pay to promote a product on television for thirty seconds during the Super Bowl? Three and a half million dollars! And why would someone pay so much money for one ad? Because it works. Have you ever bought Nikes or Adidas? Have you ever bought Howdies or Wows? What? Never heard of these last two? Wouldn't buy them, would you? We all know that name brands sell, to us and to our children, and unless we have a serious lack of money or a strong anticonsumerism viewpoint or we are tremendously independent in our thinking, we will probably buy name-brand clothes and laundry detergent and other items we see on television, hear about on radio, or see on billboards. Advertising works.

So if advertising works because it is stuff repeated over and over until it sinks into your subconscious as a wanted item, then so does other repeated stuff. Along with that, we know inputs change moods. If you want to feel energized for a round of boxing, you don't play the *Swan Lake* ballet in the background. If you want to go to sleep, Sean Paul's "Get Busy" is not going to relax you. Inspirational movies inspire, and sad movies make you feel sad. After watching *Sophie's Choice* at the theater and seeing the poor mother have to choose whether to hand over her son or daughter to the Nazis to be ushered into the gas chamber, I drove straight to Toys"R"Us and bought stuffed animals for my children. I left *Gandhi* wanting to go home and toss my excess clothes away, but after watching *Kill Bill*, I wanted to go kick ass.

Environment affects us all. As we get older and more mature, we often understand we can manipulate our environment to produce a desired result. We might paint our home in certain colors, buy a particular car, select specific music for different events (if you want to seduce a woman, what man over thirty with brains chooses heavy metal over romantic music?), and so on. Our children are likewise affected by various inputs, but they lack the ability to discern what is good and bad for them or to understand the effects of various amusements. Heck, even some adults don't understand what they are getting into when they visit chat rooms or porn sites; they may end up destroying their marriages or get into stuff better left alone, like online gambling, perversions, or overbuying on eBay. Your children are even easier targets.

The Babysitting Box

Let's start with the first invader of your child's small world: the television. When I was growing up, the shows were family fare; the television set was turned on for a specific program, not left on as background noise. It was more of a treat than a habit.

By the time my kids were growing up, many kids in the neighborhood watched a great deal of television, and some of it was not suited for their age. The television became a babysitter and an entertainer, and if parents wanted to watch something, they often didn't worry that their children were seeing a show not appropriate for kids. They simply didn't think enough about what television *is* and then take control of it.

So what *is* television? It is a visitor in your home. In olden days, much of people's entertainment came from people who came calling. Do you think proper families had pirates, prostitutes, and drunkards in their homes? Likely not, because they wouldn't want these people around their family. For that matter, do you want to have gangbangers, psychotics, perverts, killers, or someone who spouts stuff you don't agree with (racism, sexism, religious or nonreligious concepts that make you uncomfortable) spending time in your home with your kids? Of course not.

But you invite all those people into your home by way of the television; you invite them to be around your children. And a good portion of the time, you don't even know those people are there, you don't know what they are saying to your kids, and you aren't there to step in and educate your children if they hear or see something inappropriate. Considering how much television kids and teens watch, they may spend far more time with questionable people than with their own parents. And those strangers have no influence on your children? Of course they do. Lots of it.

You Should Control the Television, Not Let It Control You

So what do you do? Well, there are a number of options. You could refuse to have a television in your home. Gasp. What a concept! Actually, most of us find that hard to even fathom. I *do* have a television in my home and always have, but I am not a big watcher. I have met people who really don't have a television, and it is quite interesting to be in a place where none exists.

Okay, most of you aren't giving up television. But this doesn't mean you can't control it. The first rule, in my opinion, is no one has one in the bedroom (at least, no one but the parents). The television is in the family room, where everyone can see what is being watched. Parents decide what is to be watched and by whom. A family television also prevents children from disappearing into separate caves and living isolated from their parents and siblings. It isn't healthy for people, especially children, to spend the entire day closeted in their bedrooms watching television, listening to music, and hanging out on the Internet. They need time alone, but time locked in a bedroom with a bunch of people via electronics is not time alone; it's just a lot of time with people outside the family, often people you don't really want your kids to be hanging out with so much.

So let's say you have only one television in the living room. When do your kids watch it? That's easy: when you approve of them doing so. The rest of the time, the box stays off. I had a rule for the entire time my kids were growing up: the television was turned on only with permission. As the children got older, they would scan the TV listings looking for shows they might convince me to let them see. I remember my daughter coming to me with a request to see the British *Sherlock Holmes* series starring Jeremy Brett (it would be a weekly show). "Mummy" (I think she had turned into a Londoner), "there's a lovely new series on PBS that seems extraordinarily educational and finely acted. Might we not see this particular show?" I thought this was a pretty clever attempt to sucker me in, so she won that one. We saw the entire series, and it really was excellent.

The advantage of requiring children to request a show is that it takes effort and research on their part. Shows don't just get accidentally clicked on with the remote and then watched without awareness. Television becomes a planned activity and not a time waster and an unintentional open door to a multitude of junk that shouldn't be coming into your children's brains. Allowing your children to watch meganumbers of episodes featuring violence, gratuitous sex, profanity, rape, and depictions of gore merely "uglifies" their world and damages their view of life. You hold the key (or the remote) to what images and actions are being processed by your children. If you want them to hold certain views and attitudes, don't allow them to be bombarded with the opposite of what you wish them to absorb.

Is It Music to Your Ears Also?

Same goes for music. If it's not uplifting, why are they listening to it? It is natural to listen to a catchy song over and over and over, but understand that after a few hundred times, the meaning and content of that song is being drilled into a child's mind. Don't let your kids tell you that they just like the music and pay no attention to the lyrics. While in theory this might be true, they will hear the words anyway, and like a mantra, those words can sink in and stay in. The messages in gangsta rap and from performers like Lady Gaga are some of the worst offenders, especially if your daughter also watches the videos that go along with the music. Very few positive messages are being transmitted, and your daughter will suck that up until she starts calling her friends "hoes" and "bitches" and thinks nothing of it.

There are good choices of music in all styles: good country, good R&B, good rap, good reggae, and good gospel (well, hard to get a bad message there as long as you agree with the general religious concepts). Make sure the people singing the music and acting in the videos your daughter listens to and watches aren't being disgusting. One way to know if the music is really okay is to play the song or watch the video and put your daughter in as the artist (in your mind). If you are repulsed by what your daughter is saying or doing in your imagined scenario, then it's not okay. Using this imagery, you will find out exactly what you are comfortable with as far as your morals and beliefs go, and you will also be able to evaluate if the material is age appropriate. "The Wheels on the Bus Go 'Round and 'Round" would probably be fine for a daughter of any age to perform. However, while a love song might be fine for your seventeen-year-old to sing, it would be creepy coming out of your seven-year-old (think about those little beauty pageant girls strutting around in sexy clothes, makeup, and high heels). And would you ever be comfortable with your daughter singing anything about suicide and acting out cutting her wrists? How about songs chanting, "Kill your parents! Kill your parents!"? If you don't want your daughter laid out in a pine box or standing over you with a knife in the night, you shouldn't have her listening to that kind of extreme, mentally destructive music.

More Negative Stuff

Now that I have removed television and music from your daughter's life (and I hope you are at least smiling here, recognizing that I am presenting the strongest of views on entertainment), let me add video games and dark and dangerous books and movies. (I will address the Internet in other chapters, since this is becoming one of the biggest dangers in our teens' lives and I want to discuss its unique issues thoroughly.) Girls don't tend to be as into violent video games as boys are, but do keep in mind the concept of your daughter "living" in another dimension and having fairly realistic virtual-reality experiences in this world. Take a look at what your daughter is playing or wants to play, and be sure that there is a positive vibe to the game of good winning over evil, that women are presented as intelligent beings who have respect for themselves, and that the game does not have a ton of killing and gore that desensitizes her to the sacredness of human life. Missouri teen Alyssa Bustamante, age fifteen, strangled and stabbed her sister's little nine-year-old friend to death because she wanted to know what it was like to take someone's life.

Movies have an interesting impact on a young girl's mentality. With so much sex portrayed in them, many girls start to view sex as a gateway to excitement and glamour as opposed to the culmination of a romantic relationship. Also, it is interesting that when women are portrayed in the background of many movies, they are working as prostitutes or strippers. I can't figure out why so many movies have to have a girl swinging around a pole; if you think I am joking, start paying attention and count how many times this scenario seems to show up in today's films.

The worst of the lot are slasher movies. Slasher movies tend to be much more popular with boys (which is very frightening), and the level of misogyny and gruesome violence has increased radically; each new slasher film tries to beat out the previous slasher film for the revulsion factor. What exactly are slasher movies? They are movies from the perpetrator's point of view as he stalks his victims (almost all female) and one by one captures, brutalizes, tortures, and murders them (sometimes they are raped, sometimes not). Usually one girl gets to survive the psychopath, but the rest die horrifying and sickening deaths. Viewers are not rooting for the girls to escape (they all know the dumb blond is going to look in the basement and get chopped to bits); they are looking forward to the violent acts to be perpetrated on the young girls.

Slasher films are essentially snuff films (movies of actual rape and murder that, thankfully, are pretty rare). The only difference between one and the other is the victims in slasher films are actresses who are not really being mutilated, raped, and killed. Sadly, the actresses perform quite well, so if you didn't know it was fake, you would think you were watching a snuff film. Viewers "enjoy" the sensations and emotions of women being harmed; they will tell you they don't, but if they didn't, they wouldn't be able to stomach watching the trash. If it were from the victim's viewpoint, the moviegoers would be horrified and crying and would go home and have nightmares. They might even find it necessary to look away.

Eye for an Eye with Sally Field has one of the most horrifying serial-killer scenes I have ever seen, which shows the murder of a young teen. Kiefer Sutherland is fabulous in the role of the murdering psychopath. It is quick and stunning, and you will never forget it. While her daughter is being killed, Sally Field (the mom) is on the telephone with her, and she is going berserk, jumping out of her car in stalled rush-hour traffic, beating on people's windows to get them to call 911. By the end of the scene, you feel emotionally devastated at what the young teen went through and what her family must now live with. I recommend the film to everyone "(adults, that is)" to help you understand the horror of sexual homicide. *Eye for an Eye* may have a brutal scene in it, but what is learned from those few minutes is a positive thing, not perversion.

Where Have All the Hobbies Gone?

We have become a rather excessive society in the matter of entertainment. Once upon a time, we entertained ourselves with hobbies that seem to be almost nonexistent now (sewing, whittling, baking, making model airplanes, knitting, painting, drawing, stamp collecting, etc.). We finished our work, our school day, or our chores and then we *did* something else; our entertainment was still doing something. Now we come home from work or school, then we sit and expect to be entertained until we fall asleep. This is not a healthy choice, and we need to curtail our children's use of entertainment. The reason kids used to go out and play was that if they didn't, Mom and Dad would put them to work; no one sat around doing nothing. Children had to appear to be busy, at least playing board games with each other or doing an art project or putting together a play—something, anything, that showed they were being creative and suitably occupied. Now it seems parents aren't that concerned with what their children are busying themselves with as long as those children don't bug them. This is not parenting, it's abdicating parenting.

Don't Judge a Book by Its Cover; Check What's Inside

Let's talk about books, seemingly the most harmless of the entertainers. Yes, reading can be educational, but with a lot of the drivel out there that seems like a third grader wrote it, we could hardly call such writing "literature" or great "teaching" material. Some reading is just junk, and some is harmful junk.

Now sometimes junk can be relaxing; I confess to reading gossip magazines when I get my hair done. It is the only time I see these, so it is amusing for me to check out whose facelifts went bad, who has gotten fat, who has gotten too thin, who has hooked up with whom—hey, it's like junk food; it is okay once in a while, just not as a steady diet. Likewise, that's the way it should be with your daughter's reading material.

I always required my children to okay their reading material with me before we checked the books out at the library. I know, I sound like such a control freak, but again, who is the adult? So I let them pick things out and then I vetoed stuff I considered unacceptable for them to read. I never was fond of the R. L. Stine books for children because they always seemed like sick little preslasher movie scripts to me. I helped my kids pick out good books—I would check the book list to see what was considered good literature for their age—and then I allowed them a couple of harmless junk books for lazy reading to go with them. My daughter read all the Baby-Sitters Club books during her younger years.

By helping my kids choose good books to read, I found two things: one, they got to read fascinating stories that they learned from; and, two, they actually learned what good literature was, that it was enjoyable and even preferable to junk books. All three of my children grew up to love reading. To this day, they still read high-quality books. One trick I used to encourage reading was to require that they climb into their beds thirty minutes to an hour before bedtime. Then they had the choice to read or go to sleep early. Wouldn't you guess they always picked reading?

There are certain books I like to warn parents of girls about: anything to do with magic, witches, and vampires. These books are often considered harmless, but I question that. Yes, there are some cute books of this sort that have a good message. One of my favorites as a child was *Little Witch* by Anna Elizabeth Bennett, a very sweet story about a little girl who lived her with mother, a mean witch who turned the little girl's friends into flowerpots. The girl finally finds out that she is not a witch's daughter but the daughter of a beautiful magic sprite who is imprisoned by the witch. Happy ending, and no girl was encouraged by this book to want to be a witch.

Let's move ahead to the biggest moneymakers of recent years: the Harry Potter and Twilight series. I confess: the Harry Potter books bore me. If I had been a publisher, I would have been one of the many who turned them down and kicked myself later. My kids didn't like them, but obviously, many, many children do. I see to some extent why children (and some adults) like reading them; they just aren't my taste. I *am* bothered by some of the ideas in them, however. The humans—the muggles—are relatively stupid people to be pitied, but lucky for these special children, they aren't stuck living with them; instead they go to a creepy boarding school full of very questionable role models and classmates. It is the worst of English boarding schools with an evil bent. I could go on about other stuff in the books that gives me the willies, but I don't want to get into a religious or moral argument here; suffice it to say, pay attention to the content of the books your children are reading. Be sure you agree with it. You actually may have to read the books yourself! You may enjoy them or you may find you aren't happy with them. Either way, you will be informed about what your children are partaking of and at least be able to help them choose future books or understand something in the books you found concerning. And you can have something in common with your children and teens if you read some of the same books.

The Trouble with Twilight

Now to the other series: Twilight. These are terribly written, I must say, but I have to admit, I prefer them to the Harry Potter books. I actually *have* read all of them and seen the movies as well with my daughter. Before you think I am a total hypocrite here, my daughter and I hate the books and the movies and think the characters are all icky (except Jacob; *team Jacob!* But I digress).We read the books in morbid fascination and guffawed at the movies. Remember, my daughter is thirty years old as of the writing of this book, so she is not a young impressionable teen.

What do I find wrong with the Twilight stories? Just about everything, but especially Bella's personality,which is terribly drab, and the choices she makes, which are appalling—yet many teen girls wish they could be her. Let me dissect this.

Bella comes from a broken home, and although she loves her mother, Bella seems to view her as a kook and has little true respect for her. She doesn't seem to think much, either, of her father, who has been absent for much of her life. But she grudgingly goes to live with him for the year. So we start with disrespect for adults.

Bella arrives in Washington State, settles into her new environs, and goes to her new school. If any of you ended up changing schools as a teen, I am sure you remember how awkward it was to suddenly be the new girl (or boy) in town and have to make new friends at a school where cliques were already formed. Bella, in spite of the fact she is as drab as they come—totally devoid of personality, sullen, and annoying—makes friends immediately and has a whole group of kids adoring her and "having her back." She even has boys liking her and wanting to be her boyfriends. Yeah, right. This is fantasy. In reality, Bella would have ended up with the stoners smoking dope in the parking lot. But she gets amazingly lucky. How does she react? In a totally unappreciative way.

It seems having a really nice group of new friends does not

make Bella happy. She is just as depressed as usual and doesn't want to play any reindeer games with her pals. Instead, she gets enamored of a really disturbing, makes-my-skin-crawl, weird, pale, sickly looking dude her friends don't like. Edward Cullen, the vampire, has entered Bella's life. She also meets Jacob, the sweet-but-hot, young family friend and werewolf. Jacob adores her and offers her love and a chance of a semi-normal life in which she can at least remain a human, but no-o-o-o, Bella has to go for the creepy guy, the most dangerous and stupid choice, one that is likely to end in her early death.

Is Edward worth it? I can't see why. He has been in high school for hundreds of years. Why can't he at least go to community college and study a variety of subjects? Does a life of perpetual high school sound exciting to you? Didn't you want to get the heck out of high school by your last year? Bella doesn't even like going to school that I can see, but she doesn't see anything dreadful about hooking up with a guy who spends eternity going to twelfth grade!

Now, how about the fact that choosing Edward means she doesn't get to eat food ever again? Oh, yummy, she gets to drink animal blood forever and ever. And live with other eerie vampires who don't seem to have any fun. Forever. And, of course, the "good" vampires are in a constant terrifying battle with "bad" vampires who *can* kill you (so I guess forever isn't really forever), and they are always after Bella, which is why she needs to keep away from her family: so the vampires don't kill them along with her.

So to recap: A sullen, unattractive girl who doesn't much respect her family is willing to give it up, as well as the friends she has, to hang with a bunch of horrid vampires in an unpleasant environment drinking blood and going to high school forever, or at least until some other vampire eradicates her. Oh yeah, and she gets to be with Edward ad nauseam, and considering how short most relationships last these days, can we just imagine how pissed off Bella will be if she gets fed up with him in five years and now she is stuck being a vampire?

Is this the kind of life (or nonlife) you want your daughter to dream of? Is Bella the kind of selfish and stupid person you want your daughter to be? Do you want her to grab an Edward as soon as one shows up? I should hope not!

So why do girls go nuts over the Twilight series? My guess would be that many girls identify with Bella: they feel unattractive, unloved by their parents, and unpopular in school, and they aren't getting dates with the football players. They can relate to Bella, and then she rises above regular life because Edward chooses *her*, Bella, to love (even if he really is almost a pedophile since he has been around for hundreds of years and is taking up with a childlike, naïve girl who doesn't have much thrilling conversation to share). Oh, wait, yes, that's what these girls are hoping for: an older guy to see how special they are (they have given up on high school boys figuring it out). They just hope that by some miracle, he will swoop down and take them away from their lives (even if it means killing them in the process). They "win" by bucking the system, society, and their parents. They are finally free of the rules that aren't working in their favor.

Here is what is so dangerous about this thinking: they are not learning to accept who they are, change for the better what they can about themselves, look outside themselves to help others who have worse situations than they have, and have patience and wait for the right man. Wouldn't it be better if they could listen to their parents, value their advice, and take the time to grow up, mature, and change their lives in a positive way?

Instead, they are looking for a way to rebel, to opt out of normal life, and even opt out of life itself. Choosing life with Edward is essentially committing suicide. Much of the creepy goth stuff we see teens involving themselves with is frightening; they are embracing death, destruction, darkness, and evil rather than hope, beauty, and love. Bella becoming a vampire means she throws away her human life for something much less than God intended; it is a suicidal choice. Even worse, if she became a regular vampire, she would become a serial killer as well. Isn't that what vampires are?

Does Your Daughter Think Life Is Worth Living?

We should be teaching and showing our daughters from a young age that life is worth living, that it is a wonderful adventure, that we can achieve and experience many great things. Is it always easy going? Of course not, but we should be teaching our daughters to be strong, resilient, and to overcome frustrations and bad times. We shouldn't be encouraging them or allowing others to encourage them to toss their lives away. This is sad.

The one and only thing I can think of that is a good message in the Twilight series is that Edward waits until marriage to have sex with Bella. Of course, he is still willing to get her killed, rip her apart, and take her human life from her, but at least he isn't jumping her bones while he is dating her! Ah, how romantic! What a guy! These days girls *would* be impressed, though, by a fellow who would wait to marry them to have sex because it is so rare (oh, wait, in reality, most girls would get mad and think he really wasn't that into them or that he was gay). At least in fantasy, the girl is worth waiting for, pining for, and suffering the agony of delaying lust for. So sweet! Yes, that *is* a nice message. But I don't think the dozen negative messages along with one positive one is exactly worth the trade-off.

Dressing in all black and calling oneself the undead, a witch, a goth girl, or a vampire is a danger sign for young girls. If your daughter is dabbling in antilife thinking of any kind, get her away from it. The suicide rate for teenage girls has skyrocketed. Why? I believe it is because girls are actually viewing suicide as "cool" in a much distorted mindset that has become darker and darker over time. What a shame to lose your daughter to an early death just because she became enamored of a sick, beyond-the-grave ideology.

Your daughter's world needs to be upbeat, happy, forward thinking, and full of fun and interesting activities. She needs to see her future as full of possibility so that she looks forward to it instead of dreading it. If she thinks life is hopeless, if she views society as worthless, and if she views rebellion and the unknown as more thrilling, you may find your daughter one day hanging from the curtain rod or shot dead alongside her best friend in a suicide pact.

Feed your daughter's mind the best input you can. Review what is coming into your daughter's world through entertainment and help shape what you want her to receive. You will not likely make the same choices as I would; you will make what works for your family, culture, and religion. What is most important is that you know what your daughter is seeing and hearing and thinking about and that you make informed choices about what comes into your house and into your daughter's world.

Dear Daughter,

I hope you are not thinking I am being unreasonable or overly strict when I make sure you are watching good stuff on television or at the movies and that you are listening to nice music and playing video games that aren't too violent. Like the saying "we are what we eat," we also are what we read and watch and listen to. I want to be sure you get a lot of good stuff coming into your head, not stuff that is ugly and cruel and nasty.

All that stuff we call entertainment should be good entertainment, not junk and not disgusting. If I can watch it and an eight-year-old can watch it (or listen to it or play it), then it is probably just fine. If you have to hide the stuff when I come into the room, it might be something you don't need, either.

I want your world to be really wonderful, fun, exciting, happy, and full of love and beauty. I don't want to worry about you going over to the "dark side" and spending your time thinking about evil things like black magic, witches, demons, vampires, and the living dead. If you find yourself being sucked into that horrible place, you need to come and talk with me so we can find out why you are more interested in death than life, ugliness than beauty, and freaks than friends. There are a lot of kids these days who end up getting super depressed when they spend time with so much negative stuff—so depressed that they end up killing themselves.

I don't want you to be dragged down like that. I want you to be happy! I love you!

Two

. . . .

PARTYING, DRINKING, DRUGGING, CASUAL SEX (HOOKING UP), AND **GANGS**

They are doing too much of it—party, party, party—and at too young an age. Teens are often not mature enough to turn down opportunities that offer excitement, romance, novelty, and physical gratification, especially when their friends are involved in these activities. Too many parents think their children are wiser than they are and can handle these temptations when, in fact, too many girls are getting messed up by hanging out in places you *know* you don't want them to be and doing things you *pretend* they are not doing.

I will tell you, I am glad I am not living in a society where I am forced to marry whomever my parents select for me. I am glad I don't have to cover myself from head to toe to walk down the street and leave the house only with a male escort. I am thrilled I have the choice to work, get married or stay single, and get divorced if my partner is abusive—in other words, choose the life I want. I am glad to be free! But with freedom comes certain risks that we as parents cannot pretend don't exist.

Too Little Freedom and Too Much

Some girls live in sheltered societies with strong controls; they may have little risk of being raped by a stranger or getting into drugs or getting pregnant as a teenager. Of course, they may also be told what and when to do everything as well as suffer repression and hidden domestic abuse. There are women who are forced into marriages they abhor, are raped repeatedly by their husbands, bear more children than their bodies can tolerate, and live lives of abject misery because they do not have the freedom of choice to leave.

No life is perfect and totally free of all indignities unless one is very, very lucky. There certainly are some women who have been very fortunate to live in such cultures where, in spite of the fact that they have few legal rights, they happen to have loving fathers who picked kind, decent husbands for them, and their general circumstances are favorable and pleasing. These women might think their more controlled life is far better than a lifestyle in a country with too much freedom; they may think women in such places are forced to behave in an undignified manner, allowing themselves to be sexually used and uncared for. They could point to quite a number of examples in America, and I would be hard-pressed to deny that what they see is not exactly inspiring.

So what about your daughter? Should she have no freedom or the freedom to do anything she pleases? Should you never let her near a boy or take her to Planned Parenthood as soon as her period starts? Should you refuse to let her touch a drop of alcohol or be very European and let her drink wine with dinner? Should you ground her if you find out she is smoking herb or shrug your shoulders and say it should be legalized anyway or that you prefer weed to meth? Do you view gangs as just social clubs, or are you terrified your daughter will date a gangbanger or worse, become a gang member? As with the potentially dangerous influences I pointed out in the previous chapter, parents must decide what is acceptable and unacceptable to them as they raise their children. Again, the most important point I am making is to be aware of what is out there that might ruin your daughter's life, and I encourage you to evaluate the impact these activities might have on your particular child.

Growing Up Too Fast

We all know that kids are growing up too fast these days. They are getting adult ideas into their heads when they are still very young via a variety of conduits: the media, entertainment, school, the streets, and even their own homes. They are learning from one another. Too many of our youth are left umonitored to their own devices. They influence each other and end up with all kinds of ideas, many of which their parents would never find acceptable if they were aware of them. Some stuff that used to be unheard of in grade school children's lives is now the norm. Even some seemingly safer environments, like expensive private and religious schools, are suffering from ideas and behavior among the student population that once would have been exceedingly rare.

For example, I went to public school in New Jersey and Virginia when I was young. I don't remember even hearing about drugs except for rumors of a few kids smoking pot in the woods by the football field. I never saw a fight in the hallways. I never heard bad language. The kids who went to my high school were a fairly wealthy bunch, but I don't remember even the poorest of the group acting out. I never heard of anyone being murdered or anyone committing suicide. I don't remember a pregnancy. I thought maybe my memory just sucks, but I asked my sisters, and they don't remember much that was all that horrible, either.

As I recall, dating seemed to be put off at least until high school, and even then it tended to be toward the junior and senior years. Part of the reason may simply be that boys back in the early 1970s, when I went to school, were height- and muscle-challenged. They were short and dorky and childish-looking. (By the time my children were junior high school age, I was shocked at how many boys were, quite frankly, pretty hunky at age thirteen. They were tall and strong and quite good-looking.) So my pool of possible dates way back then were slim pickings; girls always wanted to date the older boys because they were actually taller than they were and didn't look like their little brothers. This helped keep boy-girl interactions delayed, and therefore sex was not such an issue at so young an age. Also, we didn't really know that much about sex. We didn't see it in the movies or on television, and I finally learned what I did by reading a medical book my mother had in her bedside table drawer. At age fifteen, I worked at a summer camp for the blind; when an older boy tried to kiss me, I freaked out and my mouth burned for the next thirty minutes. I thought I had done something so terribly naughty and forbidden. I remember discussing with some of the girls when we might one day have sex. One girl stated she was definitely going to have sex when she went to college, and we thought she was quite the slut for saying that!

Times have changed, and it seems like children in third grade know more than I did at sixteen. Because they see so much kissing, touching, and sex on television and in the movies, they think it's pretty normal to move ahead and start experiencing sex at a young age. School curriculums now include course materials focused on teenage pregnancy and disease, sexual practices, and the use of contraceptives—discussions that used to be left to families and their religious organizations to handle. It is no wonder that sex has become an accepted part of a teen's life and that sexual experimentation begins early. Some teens share their sexual experiences quite openly, further normalizing sex as an amusement, an expectation, a right, and a requirement. "Hooking up" has become a recreational activity for many teens.

Baby Mommies and Daddies

There is a new danger from sex these days (and I am not talking about HIV): the desire of high school girls to have babies. It used to be that getting pregnant was one of the worst things that could ever happen to a young girl. Before the 1960s, an unwed pregnant girl was whisked away to a home for unwed women to complete the pregnancy in secret and give the baby up for adoption. Then the girl would return home after her long stay with "Aunt Betty." It was quite cruel, but it was a strong deterrent to having premarital and unprotected sex. Then came the 1960s and 1970s, when "free love" and feminism took flight. Teenage girls could now partake of sex for the fun of it and run over to Planned Parenthood for birth control pills. A girl was still terrified of being pregnant, though, and if she forgot to take a pill or to use a condom, she would often get an abortion rather than have a baby. Putting right and wrong aside and not getting into an argument for or against abortion or giving babies up for adoption, one thing is clear: girls used to be very afraid of getting pregnant.

Now some *want* to get pregnant, *want* to have a baby. It has become a "cool" thing to do, and although some friends might warn a girl that being a teen mom is not a good choice, quite quickly the teen has friends touching her growing belly (now cutely called a baby bump), and then she gets a baby shower. During the pregnancy, she isn't tossed out of her school. She can walk proudly down the halls of her educational institution right until she pops. After the baby is born, she gets help with daycare from Mom or the school. There is not much punishment (outside of being stuck with a baby) that is meted out, so it is an alternative you need to be sure your daughter doesn't think is an option. It will mess up *her* life *and* the baby's, so getting pregnant is a foolish and inconsiderate thing to do.

Is Your Daughter's School Messing Her Up?

So how do you slow your kids down? Consider again what they are putting into their minds at home and at friends' houses through television, movies, the Internet, and books. Consider their schooling situation and decide if you really think that where your daughter is spending the majority of her waking hours is a place where healthy thinking and behaviors are being encouraged and expected. Of course, sometimes you have little choice over schooling if you haven't the funds to pick a better school or to homeschool. But if you think your daughter's school is a training ground for early sexual exploration and you have the ability to choose a better location, do it. The same is true for any other negative aspects of a school. If the school is full of drugs, drinking, and gangs, then work to get her the heck out of there. If your daughter hasn't committed a crime, why is she being imprisoned in a juvenile detention institution with criminals and thugs? Few parents think of a school this way, but some schools are hard to distinguish from a jail.

Hangouts

After-school environments may have similar problems. Friends' houses, malls, and parks may all be places where your daughter receives pressure from the other kids to try drugs, alcohol, and sex. Gangs also target schools and places where preteens and teens hang out (sometimes they even target grade school children) to recruit them into their ranks or sell them drugs. Temptations of all sorts are out there, cheap thrills others are raving about. How long do you think your daughter will say no if her friends are urging her to try something and she keeps hearing how awesome it is? Human beings are easily tempted to do things that feel good, give a quick and awesome high, or take them to unseen places (even if only in the disturbed synapses of their minds); in other words, these things are fun. At least, they hold the potential of fun or are fun for a while. It is kind of pointless trying to pretend these things shouldn't or don't have allure—they do. Telling your children that all these things are totally unpleasant is a lie, and they know it. They need to be educated about the long-term deleterious effects and the possible short-term disastrous and unfixable results.

Go Ahead! Have Fun!

First, let's talk about the fun aspect. Yes, these things can be quite amusing, even thrilling beyond belief. There is a reason people become addicted (or habituated) to certain drugs, and it isn't as much about the physical as the mental and emotional. No one seems to want to admit this; the politically correct thing to say is that the drug causes an immediate chemical change to the system that makes a person want to do it again. Personally, I think this is more crock than correct. If the experience was horrifically unpleasant, the chances that the person would do it again are very slim (unless she is hoping for a better trip next time). Most people are truly not physically addicted to anything just from putting it into their systems once. I know I am going to be slammed for saying that, but hear me out. What I believe truly causes people to continue drinking alcohol or doing drugs is that they like what they feel, if only for a minute. Drugs, alcohol, sex, and food change our state; they make us temporarily happier, more relaxed, more energetic, or euphoric. Changing your state the hard way, by working at it, is difficult and usually requires great patience to get to the point of the thrill. The only things I can think of that give a pretty quick thrill without having to spend a long time trying to achieve it are winning the lottery, shopping, and doing certain risky sports (flying down a hill on skis, mountain climbing, skydiving)—oh yeah, and food, drugs, alcohol, and sex. Most other stuff has to be worked on for years to reach a level of achievement that brings on a great high.

Meanwhile, your teen is being besieged with opportunities to be superexcited and happy *now*! A toke on a spliff, a tab of Ecstasy, a pretty little wine cooler—it is so easy to just go ahead and do it. Why should she say no? Well, because she truly believes it is a sin, that it will kill her or send her down a horrible path, that her parents will be devastated (and she really cares about their feelings), or that she will get arrested. Do you see how incredibly strong the deterrent must be to overcome the temptation to succumb, to miss out on a new and amazing experience, to be the odd one out of a group of friends?

Alcohol

Let's stop and take a look at the alcohol and drugs out there. For young people, drinking has gotten a lot more dangerous than it was in years past. I don't remember teens drinking that much. We didn't go to bars often. When we did, we nursed an alcoholic drink for a long time. Shots didn't exist. Martinis were not a top choice. Pretty much it was beer and a few sweet drinks; occasionally one might get tipsy and on a rare occasion accidentally drunk from carelessness.

Now the drinks are stronger, the shots keep coming, and

girls are getting trashed night after night. From bar to bar and party to party, girls are purposely drinking quantities of alcohol far in excess of what their female bodies can handle. Guys depend on this. With drunken girls comes easy sex. And there is much fear of being "roofied" these days, having some guy sneak a dose of flunitrazepam (more commonly known as Rohypnol) into a girl's drink and having sex with her while she has no awareness of what is going on. This is one reason to make sure your daughter doesn't hang out with people who can't be trusted (almost any party without adults present) or at any college bar where girls leave their drinks unattended to go dance or use the bathroom.

However, I must point out that from what I have seen, a lot of girls claim to be roofied when they are simply dead drunk. They don't want to admit they chose to drink all those shots and are responsible for their comatose state. Saying you were roofied makes you innocent of any foolish behavior. What is frightening, on the other side, is some young man being accused of something he didn't do. Here is a rule of thumb for young women: once a drink comes into your hands, hang on to it until it's finished. I would say make sure someone watches it if you need to leave the table, but I have found out too often that the person you ask to watch your drink or your purse gets distracted, so you shouldn't trust anyone in that department except perhaps a very cautious, vigilant adult.

We all know that along with drunk driving, alcohol poisoning has killed quite a few high school and college students. If your daughter is of drinking age, sit down with her and figure out how much makes her over the limit for driving, how much makes her stupid (and likely to do something she wouldn't do sober), and how much would kill her. Be sure she realizes she can do a scientific study of herself, which puts her in control of what she is doing.

As for driving while consuming alcohol, teens already can't drive worth a damn; adding alcohol, a bunch of friends, and a dark curvy road is asking for trouble. If there is truly a designated driver, that is awesome. But if the entire group has been drinking, the kids may act as though they have a combined IQ of 70. I remember how angry people became when a girl in Minnesota admitted she had been drunk when she was driving the vehicle that crashed and all the passengers were killed; she stated she felt her friends were equally as guilty because they knew she was drunk when she got behind the wheel. Furthermore, they had actually passed her a bottle of alcohol *while* she was driving. I could see where she was coming from; they were all equally responsible for the accident that got three teens killed. There was no excuse for her behavior, but there wasn't much of an excuse for theirs, either.

Because the chances are so high that your daughter may have bad consequences if she goes out drinking with friends or goes to parties where alcohol is served, I would suggest you curtail these activities, no matter what your daughter's age. It is pretty much Russian roulette when teenage girls down liquor.

Drugs

Drugs also are much stronger and more varied than years ago. Marijuana has always been around, but today's weed isn't the weak, homegrown stuff kids used to smoke because they couldn't afford Jamaican herb or Maui Wowie. It has more THC and is more potent. This means the buzz is better and more likely to get return users. Regardless of the propaganda that smoking herb and driving is a very dangerous combination, it is interesting to note that there is little research to support this opinion. Pot smokers are usually pretty paranoid that they are functioning properly, and they are likely to drive too slow or not at all rather than speed and be reckless; statistically speaking, drunk driving is the danger, not stoned driving.

But pot does cause problems for teens. First of all, it makes them slow and stupid. Yes, they are relatively docile and smile a lot, but too much pot smoking kills drive, and that is the reasons stoners are kind of useless and not contributing much to society. Also, there is a tendency for other drugs to show up around people who use and sell weed. So while it is also exaggerated that pot is a gateway drug, the problem comes with the mentality of a young person willing to try smoking marijuana and the mentalities of those already smoking it or selling it. There is a desire to rebel against society and adults, to move away from legal and healthful activities, and to be "different" in not such a really different way. The lowering of consequences for smoking pot has resulted in teens saying, "What the heck, it's not that big a deal. If I get caught, nothing that bad is going to happen that will wreck my future." Thus there is little standing in a teen's way (in his or her mind) of trying the drug. And maybe trying a second time, because it isn't that big a deal, and then again and again. By that time, a habit and a group of friends may be established, and then the future really *is* at risk.

Once one steps across the initial drug line, it is much easier to try something else. Another "what the heck . . ." because the first drug didn't kill you and was fun and opened up a new world to you, so why not something else? Gateway drugs are really barrier breakers, a testing of new waters; if you survive, then you feel more indestructible and continue.

I will confess that when I was a teen, I smoked pot a number of times. Outside of it making me laugh a lot, I cannot remember any redeeming feeling or situation that accompanied it. I remember feeling rather scummy when I did it, like

I had lowered myself to sitting around passing a joint back and forth with other people who had lowered themselves. It was an uncomfortable feeling, and, thankfully, I did it rarely, and that uncomfortable feeling kept me from wanting to do it very much in my life or to try anything else. I kept my fairly paranoid mindset that snorting cocaine one time might kill me (and I always thought it was a terribly embarrassing drug, one that had to be snorted up my nose in such an inelegant way), and I was terrified of needles in my youth (although they didn't bother me after I spent ten years working in the hospital). Oh, wait, yes, I did try speed once when I was out in Hollywood and needed to lose a few pounds for modeling. Ten minutes after I took the stuff, I started cleaning my house (something I never was good at or liked doing), didn't eat for the whole day, and zipped around like an Energizer Bunny. I never took it again because I realized that I actually loved the way I felt and didn't want to become dependent on it. Also, having my heart and blood pressure speed up like that could not be a good thing.

Speaking of speed, methamphetamines are popular for the reasons I just mentioned. People like having excess energy. You feel like you can conquer the world until you end up taking so much of the stuff that you can't sleep at night, and the overdrive becomes damaging, your hands shake, your face becomes a mess, and your teeth fall out. Meth is very alluring and very dangerous. Crack also is a road to hell. Becoming a crackhead or a meth head should be something that appalls your daughter, and she should have clear information on what lies down that road.

Ecstasy (MDMA), the club drug, alters enough of your daughter's perception to make her want to have sex with guys (and girls) she just met. The overstimulation of certain senses increases the sensuality one feels, the desire to touch and be touched. It makes one euphoric and trust people who shouldn't be trusted. That is why this drug is so dangerous in the hands of teens. It is popular in raves, so if your daughter is going to one of those, be aware that Ecstasy will be there for her to enjoy.

GHB (gamma-hydroxybutyric acid) is a party drug that some frat houses have found useful. Mixed into Gatorade, it becomes what is often called "Faderade" by college students and police officers. It is an intoxicant that some students prefer to drink, claiming they don't get a hangover with it, so it doesn't interfere with their morning classes. The problem with this concoction is that it is often made with unknown quantities of GHB, so the consumer doesn't know how much GHB is going into his or her body. It is dangerous to consume with alcohol and yet some mix GHB with liquor for added effect. Girls can quickly become easy marks when they drink too much and take GHB; it works as a date-rape drug. Your daughter may not remember too much of the evening of the party after drinking Faderade.

There are also instances of young people going into a GHB coma (it is called "g-ing out"), and friends often think it is no big deal, that their friend is passing out like a normal drunk. Unfortunately, the imbiber is carted off and dumped into bed, never to wake up. Instead of calling 911 (that would get everyone in trouble), smarter friends check the victim's breathing and turn her on her side so she won't aspirate if she vomits. Some websites for GHB users do suggest you use your own judgment (like druggies have any), and if you are worried that your friend is in danger, make sure she gets medical help. Well, that is comforting.

Unfortunately, your daughter doesn't have to rely on friends to give her drugs. She might find her own in an aerosol can (huffing), with bath salts (this is a new drug you can actually buy legally, and it is dangerous as heck), or even nutmeg from the kitchen cabinet (it has a marijuana-like effect when used in high quantity). Your daughter can go onto the Internet and look up what drugs to take and where to find them; everything anyone wants to learn about drugs and how to use and abuse them can be found online.

Are You a Druggie? Mom? Dad?

Preventing drug abuse starts at home. If you are using drugs yourself, well, it is pretty clear where your daughter might learn drugs are acceptable. Even if you use prescribed drugs like phentermine (for weight loss), you are teaching her to depend on drugs for a change of state. Phentermine is speed, even though it is not billed as that, and you can get it at "weight loss" centers. It is an amphetamine, which is why you don't feel a need to eat and why you have so much energy on the stuff. OxyContin is a drug that requires a prescription but is now popular among abusers. It should be locked up and not left around for your daughter to try or steal. Teens should be taught that drugs have their usefulness in serious medical situations, but *only* in serious medical situations.

I must mention here the overuse of Ritalin and Adderall given to children who are labeled as having ADHD. These drugs are now popular for high school and college students to help them study, to give them a competitive edge, and to help them keep on partying. They can cause dependency and heart attacks. We have a similar problem with drugs given to people with depression. These drugs used to be prescribed only by psychiatrists for patients in ongoing treatment or for patients in emergency situations like suicide attempts. Now people just tell their physicians they are bummed out, and they are given antidepressants with almost no analysis or treatment plan. Amphetamine use is rampant, and younger and younger people are put on drugs of one sort or the other by the adults in their lives (who are often using them themselves). If young people are used to legal drugs and their parents are using legal drugs, it is easier for them to slide into illegal drugs; after all, the only difference between the two is the salesman.

A Girl Needs a Family of One Kind or Another

A failing family is one of the major reasons a girl chooses to become a gang member. She can have a "home" in the gang, "sisters and brothers," and authority figures who set rules, require discipline, and demand respect. These are human needs, especially for young people. If you don't provide these needs for your daughter at home, she may find a gang to become her family and raise her for you.

If you live in an inner city, you are surrounded by gangs, maybe dozens of them. These gangs range from local crews of a few kids to the superviolent and organized ones like the Bloods, the Crips, the MS-13 (Mara Salvatrucha), 18th Street, SUR 13, Maniac Latin Disciples, Asian Boyz, Gangster Disciples, Latin Kings, Juggalos, and hundreds—yes, hundreds—more. These gangs may be national, regional, local, male, female, male and female, one race, or mixed races. Don't fool yourself into feeling safe if you live in the suburbs; my nice town just got its first gang. Even rural areas aren't safe. But clearly, the larger the numbers of youths without strong family support, the more chances there are for gangs to find new members and sustain themselves and grow. Also, there are some parents who think if their kids aren't Hispanic or African American, they are safe from gangs. This is not true; not all gangs are outgrowths of Central America, Mexico, Los Angeles, and Chicago. Many are homegrown, created right there where you live. They can be just as dangerous as bigger, more well-known gangs because they sell drugs and carry weapons just like the big boys. And while race is still an issue within and between gangs, some gangs have no racial identity, and some gangs specifically recruit members of other races and social strata to provide cover for gang activities..

Street gangs also infiltrate schools from elementary through college. Some gang members actually attend college (especially community colleges with minimal entrance requirements), and others just walk onto the open campuses. They sell drugs and recruit members wherever they go. There are a number of reasons your daughter might join a gang, including the need for protection from bullying in general or from harassment from certain gangs in her neighborhood. Or she might want to appear tough and get herself a reputation. Or she just might like to meet boys because bad boys are cool, you know. She may go there to buy drugs or to sell drugs and make money. While she is making these choices without being forced, she is still a juvenile who may not understand the long-term consequences of what she is doing.

How do you know your girl is hanging out with a gang? First of all, if you are worried that she is because of changed behaviors and friends, you are probably right. She may have a new nickname given to her by her gang friends, and she may be using slang you have never heard before, slang that is specific to one gang (the gang down the street). She may be using hand signs or scribbling graffiti on a wall on the street or in her bedroom or on paper. Graffiti is not tagging, those bubbly names you see on a wall. Gang graffiti employs symbols and numbers. If you see that, get worried. She may also wear clothing that her gang uses to identify itself, and she may get a tattoo with symbols in it. If you see any of this, go online and look up gang graffiti, clothes, symbols, hand signs, and language, and if you find something that matches your daughter's new expressions, you will know what gang she is hooked up with (unless it is a very local homegrown gang that hasn't made Google).

While you are on the computer, check her Facebook page and her friends' Facebook pages. Gang members communicate through them just like other teens, so you might get the evidence you need there. Check your daughter's room.

Personally, I don't think you should go into your daughter's bedroom or look at her diary unless you are pretty sure you have a problem with her hurting herself or others or breaking the law. Then I believe that because you are the parent, not only do you have a right, you have a duty to keep your daughter on the right road. Don't abuse your authority, but use it if you think it is a matter of life and death. If you find guns, knives, machetes, or hatchets under her bed, you have a very serious problem, and you will be glad you looked. If you find evidence of gang affiliation, be sure you don't say something to yourself like *It's a phase she's going through* or *She is just trying to impress her friends* or *I'm sure it's nothing*. It is something, believe me, something very, very serious, and you need to save her from the gang life before she ends up in prison, killing someone, or dead.

What all this sex, drinking, drugging, and gangbanging often comes down to is a lack of family life that makes her want to go elsewhere. Happy, healthy, connected teens do not end up ruining their lives with these vices. If you see your child sliding in that direction, you need to analyze what is causing this decline and take measures to improve her home, her life, and her choices. If you think you have a really great family life and your daughter shouldn't have issues with feeling loved— that she doesn't seem to be lonely, hopeless, or bored—then she may be letting curiosity and a sense of adventure carry her away. She needs your help to educate her on what traps lie out there and what they can do to her when they get hold of her.

Sometimes girls just don't realize how the world works; they are naïve and oblivious to badness and bad people. Usually that life view comes from us, the parents, so you might check and see if you too are walking around wearing rose-colored glasses or have buried your head in the sand. Don't look away from ugly things because you think recognizing their existence is being negative, cynical, or morose. Teach your daughter to learn, recognize, and avoid dangerous and illegal behavior and to make positive and better life choices. In the end, her life will be fantastic and bright (even if she knows horrible stuff exists), while the girl and her parents who put bags over their heads may find their world becoming darker and darker and uglier and uglier. I would rather know something exists than live it, wouldn't you?

Dear Daughter,

Do you remember all the fun things you used to do when you were little? Do you remember how you didn't even know about drugs, drinking, hooking up, or gangs—and you were happy? Why is it when we become teens (and, yes, I was one) we suddenly forget about all those fun things and all the other incredible things in the world we haven't yet gotten to do, and we get tempted to do things that are illegal and dangerous and stupid? I guess because it is forbidden stuff, and all human beings seem to want to check out things that are supposed to be off-limits to us.

If you are tempted to get involved with things that you know are wrong (and you do know that they are wrong), try to think about where you might end up if you mess up your mind and body with drugs and alcohol and casual sex with a bunch of guys, if you get pregnant or get HIV, if you land in jail for selling drugs, or if you get shot in a drive-by by your gang's rivals. Is that really what you dream about for your future: I can't wait to be a crackhead, I can't wait to spend time in prison, I can't wait to have babies with two or three different baby daddies? I doubt it.

I want more than that for you in life, and I know you do, too. Don't mess yourself up with things that might give you momentary pleasure but kill all pleasure in your future. Don't trade a few thrilling seconds for a miserable lifetime. If you are bored, feeling left out, or need a change, come to me and let's make a plan that you like, a plan that will bring you the excitement and connection you want. Okay?

Three

● ●

DATE **RAPE**

*E*ver since *Whoopi Goldberg* got slammed for saying date rape is not "rape rape," there has been a push to equate date rape with violent-stranger rape, and the two are *not* the same. Yes, in the end, forced sexual intercourse may have occurred, but how the attack occurred, how the victim felt during the attack, how the victim feels psychologically and physically after the attack, and the criminal-justice issues involved are very different. Date rape almost always involves alcohol and a situation or set of circumstances that are impossible to prove with success in court. This "he said, she said" crime rarely involves violence, most often involves intoxicated people (or at least one intoxicated person), and almost always boils down to the question of whether the sex was consensual. Date rape may not be as horrific or devastating as violent-stranger rape, but your daughter can have lasting issues over being date-raped (loss of self-esteem, loss of trust, pregnancy, sexually transmitted diseases), and you need to teach her how to avoid becoming one of the many teenage victims of this crime.

Why Is Date Rape So Hard to Prosecute—and Prevent?

Let me break down the issues of date rape. I am going to start at the end and work my way back to the beginning so you can see how such a crime plays out and how it can be stopped.

Imagine we are in the courtroom, which is, by the way, an extremely unlikely finish to a date-rape crime. Almost no date-rape cases end up in court, and we shall see why. Think about the Casey Anthony case, while not a date-rape crime, it was a trial with an incredible amount of solid physical evidence that was presented, and she was still found not guilty. (In case you have been living in a cave for the past few years or on the island of Tonga, you'll find the facts if you Google the case.)

Now, let's take your daughter's date-rape case before a jury. The defense attorney asks if there were signs of forced sex on the accuser, such as abrasions in the vaginal area. The answer is no. There may not even be semen because the accused used a condom or did not ejaculate. Then the defense attorney asks if the accuser went willingly with the defendant. Your daughter says she did. Then the defense attorney asks if she fought or screamed. Your daughter says no, she didn't, because she was scared. The defense attorney asks if she was scared because the accused was holding a gun to her head or a knife to her throat. Your daughter says no; she was scared because he was bigger than she. The defense attorney asks why she waited two days to go to the hospital. Your daughter says she was embarrassed.

Now the defendant is on the stand. He tells the jury that his accuser—your daughter—came on to him at a college bar, that she had him buy her drinks, and that she took him on to the dance floor, where she ground her ass against him and allowed him to kiss her and fondle her butt. Then they went to his apartment and drank more alcohol, and she took off her clothes willingly and got into bed with him. She never told him to stop any part of the sex. He says he used a condom to protect her, they had sex, she seemed fine afterward, and they parted on good terms. He was shocked that she later accused him of rape, and the accusation has made his life a living hell from that day on.

Do you think this jury would put this young college boy in prison for the next ten years on the word of your daughter alone? Do the jurors have any proof he raped your daughter? The answer is they have *no idea* if he did or did not. Quite frankly, there is zero evidence of a rape in this case except for your daughter saying that it happened. The jury cannot convict someone on an accusation without reasonable proof that the crime occurred. Does this mean a rape didn't occur? No, in reality your daughter may be telling the absolute truth, but she has no evidence to back her claim. Even if she raced to the police station or hospital right after the rape, even if the boy didn't use a condom and there was semen evidence proving he had sex with her, even if she is sobbing her eyes out, there is still *no proof* there was a rape other than the less than circumstantial "proof" that your daughter says a rape occurred.

On occasion, there might be a couple of pieces of evidence that could be presented in your daughter's favor: some sign of trauma to the vaginal or anal area and maybe some bruising to her body, like marks from fingers grabbing her arm or throat. Will that win the case in court? Not necessarily. The prosecution may put a sexual assault nurse examiner (SANE) on the stand who will tell the jury that abrasions to the vaginal area mean that the victim lacked what is called "natural human sexual response." This allows relaxation of the muscles and provides vaginal lubrication, so if the sexual act was consensual, there would be no damage to her body.

Sounds pretty reasonable, right? I can tell you the defense can tear that apart. There are reasons a girl can have abrasions, redness, and other minimal damage from consensual sex. And I am going to put out a reality that women don't like to admit and victims' advocates don't want to talk about: young women may have sex with a guy they are not that into, they may have sex they weren't prepared for, they may have sex they didn't even like or want, or they may be okay with rough sex. Sometimes the sex partner may simply suck at foreplay.

Starting with that last issue, if the guy rushes into intercourse with little warm-up (which is not that unusual with novices or drunk or disrespectful men), the woman simply is not physically ready for sex, and the penetration can end up scraping her and even causing her to bleed. It is not rape, just crappy sex.

Anal sex has become more and more popular because of rampant pornography, which these days seems to almost always ends up with a girl having anal intercourse. In most porn films, the girl can handle overly large penises in her anus with barely a whimper (likely due to excessive previous anal sex acts, but sometimes due to barbiturates that drug her up enough to be super relaxed). Your daughter could end up with a guy quite forcefully jamming his male member into a location that your daughter might have thought would be interesting to experience, not realizing it isn't as easy as he said it would be or as easy as it appeared in porn videos she herself watched. She also may not even realize his penis was going to go there; it *just* slipped in there. After the fact, she may realize that anal sex can really hurt and her butt is sore. Is this rape?

No, not if she consented to the act. It is always hard to say something is rape when to some people it is just the next sexual move. In real life, people do not constantly discuss what they are going to do next in the sexual encounter.

Finally, she may be with a guy who is so excited he kisses her once and shoves himself into her. Or he may not care whether she enjoys herself and just goes after what he wants. Or maybe once your daughter gets naked with Bozo, she realizes he doesn't really turn her on and she just sighs and gets the sex act over with as quickly as possible. Are any of these situations rape? No.

Now be honest, moms. Have you ever in your life had a less than thrilling sexual experience with your husband, boyfriend, partner, or one-night stand? My guess is you have. Sex is not always a fabulous explosion of searing joy between two people; sometimes it just blows.

All right. Now you can see why your daughter has a better chance of getting a date with Ryan Gosling or Justin Bieber than of winning a date-rape case in court. Let's back up one step now to the police station or hospital.

Date Rape and Law Enforcement

Your daughter has mustered up the courage to at least report the rape; she is to be commended for being willing to do this. But let's see what happens from the police detective's point of view.

Let's even say she's a female police detective who we believe can relate better to a rape victim than a man can.

The first thought that goes through the head of the police detective as she arrives at the hospital is, has the accuser *really* been raped? She has done interviews with alleged rape victims before and has believed some girls and not others. Now she enters the hospital examination room, where your daughter has already been given a physical and a gynecological exam, had her pubic area combed or searched for any male pubic hairs, and has had samples taken from her vagina and anus (if she says anal sex occurred). The first thing the detective will note is your daughter's demeanor. Is she a total wreck, or is she texting her friends?

You might think I am kidding here, but I am not. Behavior after the supposed crime occurred is one of the main reasons why date-rape cases stall. I worked for a decade as a sign-language interpreter for the deaf at five area hospitals (in the metro Washington, D.C., area). I interpreted many times for students of Gallaudet University (the main college in the United States for deaf higher education) who showed up in the emergency room after a night of drinking, claiming they had been raped. In ten years, I saw only one girl hysterically crying. One. This poor girl had gone to a party in a private house and had been drinking quite a lot. She was on her way to the bathroom when one of the guys—she didn't know who he was, since it was one of those parties where the house is packed with people who just show up and pay for the beer—came up behind her and shoved her into a room. It was summer; she was wearing a short dress, no hose, and panties. He shoved her to the floor, pushed her legs open, pulled her panties aside, and raped her. She didn't fight back because she was essentially a rag doll from all the liquor she had imbibed, and she was so stunned from the assault that she just lay there, dazed and stupefied, beneath him. He finished quickly, got up, spit on her, and walked out of the room, and by the time she staggered out, he was long gone and she couldn't even describe him very well.

I was in the examining room with this young woman for about three hours. The entire time, she sobbed and repeatedly signed, "I want my mommy! I want my mommy!" I did my best to comfort her, wiping away my own tears as I stood there. It still makes me cry as I write these words.

Was this girl raped? You bet. Did the case ever make it to court? No. Sadly, in spite of this actually not being a date-rape case because she never willingly went with this guy anywhere, it was still a "he said, she said" situation because college kids were screwing each other on the property, she was drunk, and there was no convincing physical damage to her body. The victim was likely warned that she had no hope for a court settlement, or the prosecutor just refused to take it. I am sure this girl felt totally betrayed by society; she was viciously raped, and she just had to go home and live with it.

But in my experience, most of the girls who came to the emergency room stating they had been dated-raped didn't fall apart in the manner of the rape victim just described. Mostly, they showed some level of being offended (How dare he?), angry (I can't believe he took advantage of me!), or annoyed (What a dick he is!). There was no sobbing or uncontrolled shaking going on. Often—and again I am not kidding—the accuser and her friend (for some reason, they often appear in pairs) go out to Denny's for breakfast when the rape test and police interview are over. To be fair, they are often hungry after being at the hospital so long and after a night of drinking, and they need something in their stomachs. I am not trying to say that if your daughter were date-raped she must cry and be very upset and have no desire to get something to eat. But if one is looking at the general manner of many girls who have supposedly been date-raped, this relative calm following the allegation is not unusual, and this is what the police detective sees when she arrives to take the report. It makes the detective increasingly skeptical of date-rape claims.

So why do so many girls who actually may have been date-raped behave this way? One, because they are still drunk; their minds are not exactly functioning well, and they are still woozy. Two, because the alcohol has dulled the vividness of the nonconsensual sexual act in the victim's mind; she was kind of out of it (or all the way out of it) when it happened. Three, because the unwanted sexual act was often one step further than the girl wanted to go, but she went willingly through the other steps. Four, because she *can't remember* if she really said no. And, five, because she is on the Pill and sexually active, so the nonconsensual act was not a horrifying affront to her virginity or to a monogamous relationship with her soon-to-be husband; it just was another sex tryst that didn't work out well.

I am not trying to be harsh or mocking; I am just being realistic. This is not the nineteenth century, when most girls were virgins until marriage. Unless your daughter is a girl with very strong religious beliefs—and is therefore much less likely to be in a date-rape situation—she may equate sex with having fun, getting a boyfriend, keeping a boyfriend, being free-spirited, or being "cool." She may just enjoy sex! If she has been sexually active, she may not be devastated by date rape, just pissed off that it happened. I am not judging girls and young women for their attitudes, but these attitudes *do* affect how the detective judges the consensual or nonconsensual nature of the alleged rape and how the jury judges the victim in court. It is not that the victim deserved to be raped; it is that it is hard to determine *whether* she has been raped when she has certain behaviors, history, and attitudes and there is no conclusive physical evidence.

Cultural Attitudes Toward Rape Victims

I have sometimes given this little exercise in training sessions to show that while we don't blatantly blame the victim for getting raped, we are influenced by the circumstances surrounding the rape. I divide the room into two groups and separate them out of hearing range. I hand out a sheet of paper that details the circumstances of a crime to each group and tell the participants to discuss the matter quietly. I ask them to come back with a verdict: Was the woman raped, and if so, what should be the sentence for the offender?

The first group always comes back and says, "Yes, the woman was raped. The offender should get maybe a year." A gasp goes out from the second group.

Then the second group says, "Yes, the woman was raped. The offender should get twenty years!" A gasp goes out from the first group.

Do you think I gave two different rape scenarios to the groups? No. I gave them exactly the same one. Confused?

Yes, the scenario is the same. The rapist pushes the woman down under him and tells her he will hurt her if she doesn't comply. He pulls off her panties and rapes her. Then he gets up and leaves.

Still confused why two groups would come back with such different sentences?

The scenarios were the same, but the victims were different.

Victim One is a prostitute working at a massage parlor. She takes her client back to the room. There she is wearing just panties, since this is going to be a topless massage. After they get on the bed, he pushes the woman down under him and tells her he will hurt her if she doesn't comply. The woman is somewhat scared, since she is not sure that he isn't a serial killer and she has not much hope of fighting him; they are on a waterbed and there's nothing much to push against. He rapes her. As he is leaving, she yells at him, "You owe me fifty dollars, you prick!" He walks out without giving her any money.

Victim Two is a Mennonite woman who volunteers teaching illiterate adults to read. A man comes to her home while her husband is there. The husband gets comfortable with the man, thinks of him as harmless, and at the fifth tutoring session, he runs to the store to get some food for dinner. As soon as he leaves, the man pushes the woman down on the couch and tells her he will hurt her if she doesn't comply. He pulls off her panties and rapes her. When he is finished, he walks out. The husband arrives home to find his wife crumpled in a ball on the floor, sobbing uncontrollably.

See the problem? The act of rape was *exactly* the same in both cases. But there is a tendency to feel horrified for the Mennonite woman, and she is completely shattered by the crime. The prostitute is only pissed that she didn't get fifty bucks. If these cases end up in court, the jury may not feel that bad for the prostitute and isn't likely to trust her word, either. The other woman was performing a public service in her home, and her husband had been there until he trusted that his wife was safe with the man; we understand that this religious married woman having consensual sex with the man while her husband was out is extremely unlikely. The prostitute, on the other hand, had sex with strangers before and after the encounter with the man she claimed raped her. So why shouldn't one believe he didn't just stiff her and that she is trying to get back at him?

Unfortunately, both cases involve a dangerous rapist, but the chance of a court convicting the one who raped the prostitute is near zero. And so it goes with date rape as well. If your daughter has a history of sexual encounters, was drinking with her date, then went someplace private with him, she is going to lose in court unless he beats the living hell out of her when he rapes her.

Was She Really Raped?

By now you are probably feeling pretty upset that the detective may be wondering if your daughter is telling the truth in this situation. You understand that without physical injuries and absolute proof of rape, the detective may not have enough to arrest the guy, much less get a prosecutor to think he or she can convict him. But why on earth would the detective doubt her claim that she was raped? After all, it takes a reasonable bit of emotional strength to put oneself through a rape exam and to have to describe what happened to a complete stranger. Here we run into two problems.

The first problem, as I mentioned before, is that sometimes the accuser doesn't even know herself if she was actually raped. She may have been so drunk that she is not sure what she actually said while she was with the guy. Did she really tell him to stop? Did she really say no? Even worse, if she said, "No," or "Stop," did she really mean it? Did the guy *know* she meant it? He may also have been drunk.

Here is where victims' advocates get their hackles up. "No means *no!*" they proclaim. If the girl utters, "No," or "Stop," she means she does not want the guy to continue. Well, in a perfect world this would be true; in the real world, not so much. Talk to enough young women and you will get admissions from some that they have said, "No, no!" and they really just wanted the guy to think they weren't so easy, they wanted to be "overridden," or they were buying time while they decided if they really wanted to go on—and then they did. Guys will tell you girls play the "no, no," game when they really mean "yes, yes." We can argue all day that this is a misrepresentation of women's behaviors promoted in lurid romance novels: "She cried out, 'Stop, my lord,' but his fingers unbuttoned her bodice and she swooned into his arms." But the fact is, some young women still don't mean exactly what they say when they say it. Young men get confused if the "No!" or "Stop!" isn't adamant enough or harsh enough or the girl doesn't make it crystal clear that she doesn't want to continue with the encounter. Add liquor and a girl who can barely move her mouth to make a coherent objection, and the sex continues. If your daughter cannot swear she made it known to the man that she wanted him to stop and that he understood what she said, the detective can't be sure any rape occurred.

False Reporting of Rape

This is an unfortunate issue that really messes things up. Some girls lie, claiming they have been raped when they have not. Yes, it does happen, and it happens more than you think. And it makes detectives cynical. Why would a young woman lie about something as serious as rape? Here's a short list:

- She is embarrassed because she had sex with someone she didn't really want to have sex with.

- She is afraid she got pregnant and doesn't want her parents to know she is sexually active.

- She got caught in the act by her mom or dad and doesn't want them to know she had consented to sex.

- She stayed out after curfew and needs an excuse for why she is late.

- She likes the attention (she is a narcissist).

- She wants to get back at her boyfriend for dumping her or seeing another girl.

- She is afraid her boyfriend will find out she cheated on him.

Here is a true story: The police were called to the residence of a woman who told the officers that she had just been raped by a friend of her husband. The woman was very upset and about seven months pregnant. When the officers asked who the guy was, she told them he was outside on the step. The officers went outside and sure enough, the guy was sitting on the step, making a phone call. They told him the pregnant lady inside said he had just raped her. The man said, "You've got to be kidding me! I didn't rape that woman!" And he proceeded to show the officers a video he had taken with his cell phone of him having sex with the woman; he was behind her, doggy style, and she obviously hadn't known he was filming the event. One thing was clear: the woman was having a very good time. The officers watched for a few minutes, started laughing, and then went back in and told the woman she would have to deal with cheating on her husband in some other way.

Cynical as detectives might be, they truly do feel sorry for girls and women who report date rape. Police officers despise rapists, and they know the harm it does to the victims. They also feel very bad when they have to tell a young woman that even though they *do* believe her, they cannot do much for her. She can file a police report, but it's likely nothing will ever come of it. They know they would hate for their own daughters to be told this after she had been date-raped. First she gets humiliated by some guy she trusted, then she gets humiliated again going through the intrusive exam and the embarrassing police interrogation, and if she ever gets to court, the defense attorney will humiliate the living hell out of her. Enough girls know that trying to press charges for date rape is only going to victimize them over and over again, so many just go home, take a shower, and hope they can forget what happened.

Date Rape Without Alcohol as a Contributor

I do want to mention that while most date rape features alcohol, there are times when a girl is totally sober and the guy may be totally sober when he forces himself on her. One advantage this victim has is that she knows for sure what happened. One disadvantage is that she remembers more clearly what happened, and it may be harder for her to deal with the crime. Physically and emotionally, non–alcohol fueled rapes by acquaintances have more in common with stranger rape in the sense that there is often a clear line of demarcation for what was consensual and what was not. In these cases, the fear level is usually ratcheted up by the rapist, or he is much stronger than the woman and can solidly pin her down. The woman is terrified, experiences the rape in vivid detail from beginning to end, and usually suffers aftereffects far more strongly than women who have experienced rape that occurs after drinking. It is also more likely that the victim was less inclined to the sexual act because she has not been partying or had her inhibitions lessened by alcohol.

Does this mean nonalcohol date- or acquaintance-rape victims have a better chance of being believed and getting the rapist prosecuted? Not much better, I am sorry to say. It's still a "he said, she said" situation, and although the woman's claim might seem somewhat more likely than if she was drinking, the jury still has to eliminate the possibility she is just lying, and how does it do that? Usually, the man has to confess and although on occasion he might brag enough to get himself convicted, it is a very rare occurrence.

So What Should Girls Do?

Well, have I thoroughly depressed you? Have I slapped down all the fine efforts made by colleges and advocates who try to help young women stand up against their rapists and report date rape? Am I saying high school and college girls should stop having fun, never go to a bar, never drink alcohol, and never go on a date? Always have a chaperone when they're with a young man? Wear a burka and only see men when they have a male relative along? Actually, doing all of this would decrease date rape dramatically, but I doubt many young women would want such restrictions, and more realistically, few would follow them. Families with strong religious beliefs and rules on dating may already find the likelihood of date rape much lower for their daughters, but they should keep acquaintance rape in mind. Your daughter doesn't have to be on a date to get raped by someone she knows; it can simply be a male friend she is studying with, a workmate, or a church friend. Acquaintance rape is more difficult to prevent because this really means limiting your daughter's time alone with any man. Some families have strict rules about their daughters being alone with a man; this is a decision your family will have to make.

Let's look at ways that can help minimize the danger of date and acquaintance rape and what you need to talk to your daughter about.

Since drinking and dating make up the majority of date-rape scenarios, I will focus on this first.

Rule Number One: You need to teach your daughter that she should never go alone *to* any place or end up alone with any young man *in* any place where sex is likely to occur *unless* she plans to have sex with him. These would include his room, her room, an empty spare room in someone's house, the backseat of a vehicle or the back of a van, and a green pasture. Any man can tell you that the main purpose of getting a girl alone is to have sex with her. Okay, I am being unfair; maybe *some* guys just want to talk to or court a girl, but let's face it, most of the time when a man starts plying a young woman with liquor, one can conclude he probably doesn't have pure intentions. And once she is alone with him, she rolls the dice; she might get a lucky seven or she might roll snake eyes. If she hasn't known the young man she is with for a very long time and he hasn't always shown the utmost respect toward her, she is taking a gamble on what might happen next.

Rule Number Two: The first drink makes you stupid. How many diets have been ruined by having "just one" glass of wine? You enter the Italian restaurant with a plan to have a salad and just one piece of bread. Then you start sipping a nice glass of Chianti, and before you know it you have had two glasses of Chianti, five pieces of bread with olive oil, the salad, a massive plate of lasagna, and a piece of chocolate cheesecake for dessert.

Alcohol turns one little kiss into a lot of groping, and suddenly clothes are coming off. The author Dorothy Parker has a famous quote that comes to mind. When she and friends had joked about alcoholic drinks putting one under the table, she commented, "One more drink and I'd have been under the host."

And that is just where your daughter will end up if she drinks too much: under some guy she hadn't planned to be under. Teach her that alcohol is safe to drink only if you are in a safe location with caring people who will protect you from any harm. Fraternity houses, bars, parking lots, basements, and parties with no adult supervision are places where your daughter is unlikely to have anyone looking after her best interests. Even her best girlfriends may not always be there as they promised; they may get drunk, too, and run off after guys for their own fun.

Rule Number Three: Teach your girl to stop and think about how a guy like that picks his prey. Date rapists are often serial date rapists; they are proficient at their crime and at picking the best victims. Ask her to imagine a bar or a party where all the girls in one of her classes end up. Ask her which girls she thinks the young sex predator will move in on, chat up, and buy drinks for. Ask her which girls she thinks might end up drinking too much and going off with the guy to some isolated spot for a chat, a kiss, a little romancing.

Watch how quickly she puts girls in the high-risk category, the medium-risk category, and the low-risk category. Then ask her to figure out where she fits (you can tell her she doesn't have to tell you). Being in one category or another doesn't make her a good girl or a bad girl, but Mr. Date Rapist likes it when the girl he is most likely to get what he wants from isn't likely to report him or, if she does, won't be believed. Teach her to stop and look at herself as men do, and then she might realize she needs to avoid doing anything that makes them want to target her. Encourage her to be a profiler when she is out among young men, to be proactive. Once she starts seeing how certain behaviors spell trouble and how guys treat her, she will be able to make better choices, turning her into a smart operator rather than a hapless victim.

Rule Number Four: If you think she isn't old enough or wise enough to understand what her behavior might get her into, then she is not old enough to be left to her own defenses. Remember, as her parent you must decide what a reasonably safe choice of activities is for her. You might have to simply not allow her to go certain places or associate with certain people. You might have to restrict certain freedoms in high school or even in college (if you are paying for it). It is worth the extra effort to ensure that your daughter isn't running wild. If she ends up date-raped, the effect it will have on her life is going to be a lot worse than telling her she can't attend a party with people who are questionable or go on dates when she is far too immature to handle intimate situations with men.

Date rape might not be "rape rape" of the ultraviolent sort Whoopi Goldberg was trying to distinguish it from, but it is still rape, and being raped is no picnic for any woman.

Dear Daughter,

You probably have heard a lot at school about date rape and acquaintance rape, about how a guy you thought was okay might take advantage of you when the two of you are alone. You might have heard that "No!" means "No!" and how if he forces sex on you in any way and doesn't stop when you want him to, he has raped you. You will hear how it doesn't matter if you have been drinking or were willing to have some sort of sexual fun with the guy or if you willingly went with him to be alone. They'll tell you that if he initiates a sexual act you didn't want, you should report him to the police.

What you need to know, however, is that most of the girls who report the crime to the police don't actually see anything happen to the guy who raped them. If you go with a guy to be alone with him, he can say you went to have consensual sex. If you say he did more than you wanted and you said, "No!", he will say that is not true and that you never told him to stop. It will be his word against yours, and no court of law will convict him because you say he wronged you. Date rape is a crime, but proving the guy committed the crime is very, very difficult.

Be careful when you are with a man. Don't go with him to an isolated place if you haven't known him for a long time and know that he really respects you. Don't get drunk with guys you don't know at a party or a bar or with friends; alcohol makes you stupid and careless, and the guy who is looking for a girl to rape looks for the girl who isn't thinking clearly, who is giggling and flirting and willing to take a little risk to have fun. Suddenly you will find that guy on top of you, and you won't be able to push him off because he is bigger and you are weaker (and maybe really weak from drinking). After he has sex with you and sends you home, you will have to decide whether you want to try to prove to the police that you were raped, or you will end up having to be a quiet rape victim who tries to pretend what happened wasn't really that bad. You will have to make sure he didn't get you pregnant or give you a disease.

Date rape is a crime, but it is one of the easiest crimes to get away with because it is so often impossible to prove. Please come to me and talk with me about how you can keep safe from men who are looking to take advantage of you. And, God forbid, if it ever happens that you do get raped by a date or a male acquaintance, come to me so that I can help you decide what to do and get you all the help and support you need.

Four

. . . .

THE **DANGERS** OF **SOCIAL NETWORKING** AND THE **INTERNET**

T *he Internet, cell phones, texting,* Facebook, Twitter, Myspace, and chat rooms are all great ways to expand your knowledge, enlarge your social circles, and connect with friends. They are also great ways to get bullied, stalked, humiliated, and sucked into bad situations and unhealthy thinking and interests. If you wouldn't let your daughter walk into a porn video store or hang out with lowlifes down on the corner, she shouldn't be involved with such ideas or people in the virtual reality world, either. You need to monitor her activities even if she doesn't like it. The Internet is a dangerous place where not only can she interact with people she shouldn't, but also be lured to sites that can damage her psyche and modify her behavior for the worse.

Free Porn!

Pornhub.com. If you just read that site name with your mate, your son, and your daughter looking over your shoulder, and you don't recognize the Web address, you may be the only one who doesn't. If you look around and see smirks on the others' faces, you know you are the naïve one in your family.

If you think I have let some cat out of the bag, don't get too mad at me. All your daughter has to do is Google a few naughty sex words and that site and a dozen like it will pop up in her search. One day I put the word "Batman" into the image search because I wanted to find a cute picture for a kid I knew—and I got a photo of someone dressed in a Batman costume, crotch cut out, getting a blow job. Isn't that a nice thing for your child to stumble across? Make sure you have adult content blocked at the top level on any computer your impressionable kids can access (even if that means my organization, the Sexual Homicide Exchange, won't show up). It is worth keeping a lockdown on porn because you never know when your child will put in "horse" and come up with a woman having sex with one.

I am leaping right into Internet pornography because this is what runs a good portion of the Web and makes an incredible amount of money (for certain people). And it is nearly impossible to keep pornography out of your daughter's life unless you work to keep it out. The early days of the World Wide Web hinted that porn was going to increase exponentially over time in the new medium. It started out with tightly controlled websites that required a credit card to purchase entry and view photos and videos. It was hard-core porn, but not always of the vilest sort, and it cost money. Mostly it was husbands who got in trouble when their wives saw odd charges on their credit card bills with peculiar company names.

And *those* were the good old days. Pornography is rampant on the Internet now, and one doesn't even need a credit card to purchase viewing time. Present-day porn sites offer amateur and professionally made pornography for free. Thirty-minute hard-core porn videos of every sort of sexual act, including bestiality, incest, sadism, bondage, paraphilia (perversions of all sorts), "little Lolitas" (girls who look younger than eighteen with older men, even though they are of legal age), and an incredible amount of degrading and violent sexual abuse of women.

Being aware that pornography exists, and the extent of its reach and depravity, is to be educated. Making decisions on curtailing or blocking its inroads into your daughter's life is smart. Helping her become educated and wise is your duty. While your daughter is unlikely to be as attracted to pornography as your son is, it still can be enticing to explore, and its impact on her and the boys she meets is substantial in today's world.

What's Love Got to Do with It? Absolutely Nothing

Pornography has three roads of negative influence in your daughter's life: how young men and women think about sex, romance, and self-worth in general; how it influences your daughter's romantic and sexual relationships with men; and its use as a gateway drug into the sex trade.

First, let's look at what porn does to one's attitude about the other sex. I can tell you straight up, it degrades women and makes them sluts, bitches, and hoes in the eyes of boys who have watched too much of this stuff. Girls who have seen porn may see themselves in those roles. Romance is hard to maintain when disrespectful sexual acts are encouraged or forced on young women. Self-respect slides downhill, both for the girl and for the boy she should be proud of. He becomes a user, she becomes the used, and the beauty of romance and love dissipates very rapidly. It is a terrible shame to see thirteen- and fourteen-year-old girls who view sex as a commodity and deprive themselves of experiencing true romance and lovemaking.

I remember a young man of sixteen who called in to a radio show because his fifteen-year-old girlfriend asked him to tie her up and whip her. He was repulsed by the idea, but she thought him a goody-two-shoes with limited sexual experience because he didn't want to get rough and manhandle her. Maybe she had been sexually abused early on, but you might be surprised how many young girls now think rough or degrading sex is normal sex and that they should indulge in it to make a guy happy.

Young women also need to think about what an early and unromantic dive into sex means for their future relationships. It is pretty well-known that talk goes around among the guys (and even the girls) about what your daughter will do with whom and how many she has done it with. Getting labeled a slut does not exactly bode well for having guys treat her well. Also, when she enters the next relationship, she brings with her sexual behaviors that may immediately tell the boy that this girl has been around the block a few times. Some guys think this is no big deal and that in this day and age, a girl shouldn't be expected to have less sexual experience than a guy. Well, maybe some guys think this, but not many. Reputation is still something that exists, and a girl with a "bad reputation" tends to be treated with much less respect than a girl whose name isn't hooked up sexually with a number of young men.

In reality, it has never been healthy for either partner in a relationship to have a spreadsheet of previous bedmates that the new person has to compete with and imagine their beloved doing everything they are doing with someone else. Not only that, when the couple runs into old sex partners, it is a bit unsettling to know the person standing in front of you has seen your boyfriend or girlfriend naked and has had sex with him or her. Sure, sometimes one has to deal with these things, but it helps to avoid going down a road filled with a variety of road bumps and slippery pavement.

We're Just Talking

Along the porn highway lies another very dangerous road condition: the chat room. Many of you have likely seen the famous *Dateline NBC* show, *To Catch a Predator,* in which trained adults pose as teen girls and enter discussions with men in various chat rooms, or men who pose as teen boys. Each show features a number of men who have each made a date to meets the girl he has been chatting with online. He shows up and meet the girl (an actress), and then she leaves the room and Chris Hansen walks in. He has a polite but pointed conversation with the predator about what the man was planning to do with the young girl. He points out that the man knew the

girl was only thirteen or fourteen years old. The sexual predator usually lies and, in spite of the evidence—bringing along
condoms, alcohol, and sex toys and having a recorded discussion about sex with the girl *after* he learned her age—claims
he only came to help the teen with her homework or to be her
friend! Then the film crew rolls into the room with their big
camera and he flees, only to be arrested by the police as soon
as he gets out the door. What is particularly striking about the
show is that most of the men seem fairly docile, friendly, polite,
and even kind of like a nice neighbor. But sexual predators they
are, and they all lie like dogs, give the same bogus excuses and
justifications, and want sex, usually oral and anal sex along
with the hope of deflowering a virgin if they can get it.

These sexual predators spend an inordinate amount of time
on the Internet, viewing pornography to stoke their desires,
and in chat rooms, trying to talk sex with teenage girls. They
hope to get lucky and eventually meet the girls and have sex
with them. Barring that opportunity, they will masturbate
while they talk dirty to the girl, send her pictures of their private parts, and ask for photos of her. A man may attempt to
get a girl to masturbate and tell him how she is enjoying it,
or even to commit sex acts with others and come back and
report. He may also coerce her into turning on her webcam
and then watch her do things to herself.

Most sexual predators only appear to be clever because

they troll for inexperienced teens who will fall for their well-practiced ruses. You may wonder how smart these men must be to rope a young girl into a sexual relationship with them, even if they never meet in person. You may have heard how incredibly charming psychopaths are, and you may think the man must spend a lot of time online "grooming" a girl before he starts talking sex to her; that he first must become her friend and then slowly introduce sexual comments into the conversation.

Not true. In reality, most of these psychopaths haven't got a lot of patience—one trait of a psychopath is the inability to set long-term goals, and another is impulsiveness. Most aren't going to waste valuable time chatting up some girl for weeks in the hope she will eventually give him what he wants. No, the conversation your daughter could get into with one of these creeps in a chat room will devolve very quickly into sex talk. If it doesn't, he will focus on one of the other open chat windows he has going (sometimes a dozen at a time) that is more promising. While he may start with some generally friendly and benign comments and questions like "Hey, hi, this is Paul, what's your name? How old are you? Are you doing your homework? No, heh, listening to music? Kewl. What's your favorite rapper? Yeah, I like him too. So are you home all alone? Yeah, me, too. I am just hanging out playing some riffs on my guitar. Do you have a boyfriend?"

Can you see where this conversation is going? Pretty soon, he is going to be asking her if she is a virgin and what kind of sex she likes to engage in with her boyfriend. He will tell her how he would like to "teach" her how to have great sex and please a man. (It is very disturbing how many sexual predators use the word "teach," as if this makes them a good guy just trying to help a girl along the path of education.)

So if it is so obvious so quickly that the guy is interested in sex and not friendship or any other particular interests your daughter may have, why would she not just shut him down and get out of the chat? Unfortunately, it is because she is excited by the discussion. Don't forget how hormones rage in the teen years, how curiosity about sex is overwhelming, how tantalizing it is for teenagers to experiment with the unknown, the forbidden, and the only-for-adults activities. And here she is, in her bedroom all alone *with a man* and most likely, as she is probably well aware, an *older* man. She can explore talking about "dirty" things and no one will know. An older man is paying attention to her, treating her more like an adult, offering her forbidden fruit. It is very alluring, and she may not realize, as she delays hitting the X at the corner of the chat box and answers just a few more questions, that she is getting drawn in and more involved with the titillation of what she is doing and what the man is doing with her.

An interesting psychological state akin to Stockholm syndrome develops between your daughter and the pervert she chats with. Stockholm syndrome is what often happens when a victim is imprisoned a long time by her captor; he becomes a real person to her, a "friend," and a relationship is established. Don't think that just because your daughter isn't trapped in the man's basement and she doesn't really know who he is, maybe not even what he looks like, that this kind of relationship isn't occurring. He has become an ongoing part of her daily life. Remember how in the old days many a romance leading to marriage flourished through letters exchanged by complete strangers? Likewise, today, relationships are forged on dating sites through e-mails and chats and on Facebook and Twitter. When those relationships end, many people will feel oddly bereft and upset at the loss of the Internet friend. The emotions are the same whether you see the person in front of you or you communicate with him halfway around the world via the Internet. Sometimes people even feel sad when they wake up in the morning and "lose" the person they were spending time with in their dreams.

Her Online "Friend"

Every minute your daughter spends with a sexual predator online is another minute she is becoming attached to him emotionally, which means he has a better chance of talking her into more sexual acts or possibly meeting him. Part of her thrill in hooking up with him online or in person is a bit of rebellion and dangerous adventure that she is pulling off behind her parents' backs. And like other addictions—drug addiction, for example—higher levels of stimulation are needed as she continues to involve herself in the addicting habit. She will return to her computer day after day, night after night, to see if her "friend" will pop up and they can play at the next level, whatever it is. Her friend is like a box of chocolates she is not supposed to know about or touch that is hidden in the back of a drawer in the kitchen: she is drawn to want it, so she sneaks into the kitchen when no one is around, slides that drawer open, and carefully removes one of the chocolates, all the time hoping she will not get caught.

Her secret sexual relationship on the Internet is just like that, only far more damaging than a few calories from stolen candy. She may realize, at some point, that what she is doing is humiliating and wish she could take back everything. It doesn't matter that you later tell her that a grown man was manipulating her; she will still feel like a fool, and what she did may trouble her for a long time. Worse, what if anything she did got out in the community? What if pictures or videos she shared end up on the Internet for all her friends and family to see? What if her "friend" starts threatening her with exposure of these materials if she doesn't do everything he asks?

What if she ends up meeting him and the virtual becomes real and physical? Some of these creeps may "simply" have sex with her, use a condom, and leave her more "educated" but not pregnant or diseased. Others may not be so "decent," and she could suffer lifelong repercussions. At worst, he might kill her if he fears she will go to the police and rat him out. What may have started as just a peek into Pandora's box online may end in catastrophe.

Make sure she is not able to access these kinds of chat rooms on the computer in your house.

Sick Sites

Along with pornography on the Internet, there are other dark places your daughter shouldn't be visiting. On the Internet, there are sites for just about any bizarre idea, practice, or philosophy you can imagine. There are gaming areas in which a teen can role-play, for example, taking on a persona that doesn't jibe with any of the qualities she possesses in real life. It can be fun, but it can also get out of hand. Remember, even adults can become overly enamored by the virtual world. Many of us know we spend too many hours surfing the Internet and spending time on our laptops instead of being involved in other pursuits that might add more quality to our lives.

Lest you think I wouldn't touch anything on the Internet,

I can assure you I've found a lot of success and amusement through my use of blogs, Facebook, Twitter, and online Scrabble (I am a tournament player). I have built my business and educated people about profiling through my websites and blogs online. I love to Google, and doing so has filled in a good deal of my knowledge gaps. I make my travel arrangements in a flash online, and I can be my own physician a good deal of the time by studying medical issues. I like the Internet, but I also recognize its dangers: negative inputs, unhealthy associations, the chance of being harassed and stalked, and wasted time when I get distracted or want to procrastinate.

If your daughter is wasting too much time and not getting her homework done or shunning friends for a virtual world, then she is spending too much time online. If she doesn't come out of her room for hours, and she identifies more with a fantasy world where she is a superbeing than with real life, then she is overdoing it. And if she is intrigued by sites on the net that are bizarre, you need to get in between her and the computer. What am I talking about? She could be exploring sites praising the Columbine shooters, or she could be on a gore site, getting deeper and deeper into mutilation of the human body. She could be in a cannibal chat room. Yes, there is such a thing!

A famous and gruesome case out of Germany was the result of two men who met in such a place, a website called the Cannibal Café. One of them, Armin Meiwes, was into being the cannibal, and the other, Bernd Brandes, got into the role of being eaten. A sort of sadomasochistic relationship developed that finally reached a crescendo when they decided they had to play out their fantasy for real. The victim boarded a train and traveled to the cannibal-to-be's town. Once there, he took a drug to make himself relaxed. Then, filming his actions, the cannibal started cutting pieces off his victim's body. Finally, he killed the man, chopped him up, packaged sections of him for the freezer, and cooked part of him. He then set the table and ate his human dinner while drinking a fine wine. He was eventually arrested, was convicted of manslaughter, and received an eight-year prison sentence. He was then retried and found guilty of murder and will be behind bars for life.

I am not telling you this story to nauseate you, but if you are feeling a bit squeamish, just think how you will feel if you find your daughter has a log-in at that cannibal site with the name "IamYummy." There are sites that encourage homicide, sites that encourage suicide, and sites that promote terrorism; if you can think of it, you can find it online. Even if you can't think of it, you may accidentally find it, or your daughter may; and she could become a victim of whatever ideology is being spouted there.

Social and Antisocial Networks

Let's talk about the world of social networking, in which your daughter is actually chatting with friends via Facebook, Twitter, her iPhone, or her iPad, her BlackBerry. Because social networking is now instantly available on portable devices, she doesn't even have to be at home on the computer; she can be chatting anywhere, even at school. She can send pictures, too. I am sure most people have heard of the problem with "sexting," girls sending pictures of themselves, naked or nearly naked, via text message.

Most of the time, what is going on is harmless: friends talking to friends. It is fun to know where your friends are and what they are doing, and it is fun to share your day with them as well. But there is a downside to social networking, which has become a big problem: the increasing incidents of harassment and bullying.

To Be or Not to Be Bullied

There have always been kids who are bullies. Certainly, throughout the years, some children have dreaded walking to and from school because they ran the risk of getting picked on and beaten up. Some even joined gangs just to have protection. In areas with an increased diversity of cultures and religions (and sexual orientation), there are new animosities as students find themselves not understanding the behaviors, thinking, or cultural mores of their classmates.

These frustrations, along with general juvenile nastiness, cliques, gangs, and popularity battles have caused an increase in students being cruelly targeted for abuse. Pay attention to your daughter's behavior and mood, and *listen to her* if she says she is being harassed on the bus, on the walk to school, in the halls or the lunchroom, or during class. Be sure you have good communication with her about the atmosphere at school and how she is getting along with and being treated by other students. If there are problems, you need to find out if it is she, the other students, or a combination that is causing the issues. Then those issues need to be resolved. If your daughter is excessively whining about normal imperfect teens at school, then she needs to improve her attitude and learn to deal with life. However, if what she is telling you is that she is terrified to go to school or that the attacks on her are destroying her self-esteem to the point that she is becoming seriously depressed, then she—and you—must take action.

What action can be taken? First, the two of you need to sit down and discern whether your daughter's own behavior, the clothes she wears, and the things she says are the root of the problem. The idea that we all should be free to look and act any way we please and that no one should be negative about it is both idealistic and a bit self-centered. We all are members of groups, and we have to conform to a reasonable extent so as not to make other people uncomfortable or provoke retaliation. Each group has variables on what is acceptable and what is not as well as and how much leeway one has before the line is crossed and one will get a strong negative reaction.

Example One: Your daughter goes to school dressed like, in essence, a streetwalker and gets called a hoe and then comes home crying to you. You shouldn't be marching down to the school to complain that your daughter is being called bad names; you and your daughter should be discussing appropriate dress.

Example Two: Your daughter goes to school wearing clothes that look like she lives in the Little House on the Prairie—but she attends school in a posh suburb. If the granny look isn't superpopular at the time and students are making fun of her, you need to update her clothing.

I am not saying your daughter shouldn't express herself with her own style, but you need to evaluate just how much heat she is going to take for it and tone it down if it is an issue. She will be treated better, and she won't instigate bad behavior on the part of the other students. You can also help her understand that school is not the only place to express herself; in fact, it is a place to receive an education, which is the priority; socializing and expressing herself are lower on the list. She can always express herself elsewhere. If she likes wearing granny clothes, she can work on a colonial farm as a volunteer and dress the part. If she wants to wear bizarre clothes, perhaps acting or modern-dance classes will fit the bill.

Example Three: Dressing goth or in Columbine-style long, dark coats with boots is probably going to push your daughter into the freak group. Not only is it a negative group to be in, she is also going to be considered some kind of messed-up emo (emotionally overwrought kid wearing her angry, antisocial, disconnected personality on her sleeve). Some teens may argue that this is not at all what such clothes and behavior mean, but, in fact, it isn't a stretch to see that goth is not a particularly inspiring persona for any teen to be exhibiting. Quite a few teachers and students find themselves uncomfortable with this kind of group, wondering if its members have homicidal or suicidal ideations rolling around in their heads. It is not fair to frighten the people around you, and parents should not support this kind of behavior in the home or at school. If your daughter is in this mode, she needs guidance, not a thumbs-up.

Help Your Daughter Change or Change Things for Your Daughter

Being weird, too weird, or too far outside the comfort zone of the main group can contribute to harassment and bullying. Work on making sure this is not the issue for your daughter and help her adjust how she presents herself at school. If she can't do this, find a schooling situation that suits her better (like an art school, a school overseas, or homeschooling); make your daughter's life better and set her on a road to success. There is nothing wrong with making a major change if it would be advantageous to your child.

I had a friend whose son was seriously geeky and was not doing well in public school. His parents hemmed and hawed for a couple of years over homeschooling him and then finally decided to give it a shot. It turned out to be the best thing they had ever done.

One of my sons was enrolled in an American college, and I felt he wasn't doing that well; he wasn't challenged enough. I sent him to India for the last year of his bachelor's degree in economics, which he actually earned at the graduate school of a top university. The university was very, very tough; every exam required students to walk in the door with a sheaf of paper and a pencil, and the professor wrote a series of essay questions on the chalkboard. If you didn't know your stuff, you failed. My son ended up having a supersuccessful final year of college with very high grades, and he got to live in a different culture and travel around a fascinating country as well. I was very happy I'd made what seemed a bit of a crazy decision to send him overseas instead of just letting things go on as they were.

Help your daughter do well in the school she is in or move her out.

Social-Network Snakes

What about the harassment and bullying we hear about with social networking? Is this more of a problem than what happens in school, is it separate from school, or is it just adding to the stress of your daughter's problems there? I would say that for the most part, social networking is an extension of the social circle she is hooked up with on a daily basis. In other words, the cliques at school and the bullies at school now have continued access to your daughter when the final bell rings at the end of the school day. They may "follow" her home on her phone and slither into her bedroom via her Facebook page.

In the past, the only way mean kids could get at your daughter once she walked off the school grounds would be to find her at a teen hangout or call the house on the family phone. That kind of contact is easier to prevent than when the bullies can access your daughter electronically and tear her down. Of course, if your daughter doesn't have any access to electronics, this is the end of the problem. But since most girls do, if your daughter is one of them, you need to realize just how aggressive some of these haters can be and why your daughter is finding it hard to ignore them.

Visibility is a factor. Before the Internet, cell phones, and smartphones, if a group of kids was gossiping about you, you didn't hear it. Oh, you might hear about it *later* from a friend (who may not be much of one if she is bringing you that information), but it wasn't in your face. Before blogs, Facebook, and Twitter became popular on the Internet, I got an occasional hate e-mail from someone who saw me on television and didn't like what I had to say. I remember feeling shocked that someone would write something so horrible about me; for example, "I saw you on FOX this morning and you said some things that made me stop and think. Then I realized you were a complete idiot and you look so manly, I guess you have created a sexless gender." Heh! I have learned to laugh when I see stuff like this now, but I remember feeling the blow to the gut when this kind of nasty message arrived in my inbox, and it bugged me for days. Your daughter is just a teen, and this kind of meanness is much more difficult for her to evaluate properly so she can put the comment where it belongs—in the "Stalker and Nutcase" file.

Today I look back and think how nice it was when I got just a poison e-mail every once in a while. With the advent of so much social media, I now have hate blogs dedicated to me as well as Facebook hate pages. There are "hate tweets" spewed out at me (sometimes every minute) by some obsessed stranger out there in cyberspace. I feel a bit like a stand-up comic on a bad night, getting booed, and having tomatoes thrown at me. You have to have a very strong sense of self or purpose and a good understanding of psychology to accept why some people make it their life's work to harass you on the

Internet. There was one woman in particular who spent years posting nasty comments, day and night, on any blog she could find about me (including my own) and then started claiming that I was her stalker dedicating her Myspace page and Twitter to spreading the lie! She harassed and bullied other professionals and authors, too, and became a real menace.

Sadly, the Internet has very few controls, so stopping vicious bullies is nearly impossible from a legal standpoint. It is pretty much the Wild Wild West, and if you go out into it you may get shot at or shot down, and no one will do anything about it. You can't tell Facebook and Twitter that people are being mean to you or defaming you; they won't get in the middle of millions of people's squabbles.

Harnessing the Harassment

Let me tell you how I have dealt with some of this harassment; the ideas may help your daughter. Then I will talk specifically about the teenage world of social-media bullying, because that is a bit different from what adults have to deal with. My bullies are not people I know from my own community and real life. These are people out there in the Internet world; so I am lucky they don't intersect with my physical life —at least none have done so yet.

How do I deal with attacks? The best way is simply to ignore them. These bullies want to be recognized, to know you are upset, that they are making you cry and are freaking you out. They want you to feel humiliated when they cut you down. They often look for a weak spot to exaggerate and harp on or find some way to damage your reputation in such a way that people might start believing their assertions. Bullies want to know you are paying attention to what they say and that other people are paying attention to them, too. They like to know they are getting to you.

Ignoring them weakens their power over you and keeps you from focusing on the negative things being said about you. If you don't hear bad stuff, you don't think bad stuff. Some celebrities wisely have assistants who block all negative communications so that attacks don't become emotionally debilitating. I don't have an assistant to do this, so I have to figure out how to block the stuff myself and decide what I want to see and what I don't. I block people who say garbage about me on my Facebook page; it is my page and I find it rather incredible that someone even thinks he or she has the right to come into my house, so to speak, and be rude to me. So say something nasty, and I toss you off my page. People accuse me of preventing freedom of speech, but that is ridiculous. Folks have the right to speak up on an open forum or on their own pages, but they don't have the right to come *to* me and be abusive. I do not have to tolerate that.

If these people become a major and ongoing problem, I might choose to click the comment moderation button and screen the comments before I allow them up. I may have to see them, but at least I know no one else will see them, and that can be a relief. Of course, on Twitter, it doesn't quite work that way. You can block people, but that only means you won't see the nasty stuff they write about you; other people will still see it. But like a block on Facebook, where you won't see their pages or what they post, if you don't see the junk, you can forget these people even exist and that slurs are being written about you. It's kind of like those people gossiping behind your back; no, it isn't nice, but if you don't know it, at least you don't have to deal with it all the time.

This may seem like a simple concept, but it is surprising how often it doesn't occur to people and how hard it is for them not to *want* to know what is being said, even if it is not healthy to know. But this is something you control. You can't stop people from talking, but you can stop listening! So can your daughter, but she will need encouragement and support to break her compulsion to have to know what others are saying about her.

How do you stop caring what these people think? The easiest way is to ask yourself who these people are and why anything they say matters. There are two groups that should matter: people you respect and care about, and people you have regular important interactions with (whether you like it or not—your boss, your coworkers, other students, and teachers). If the people really matter, then there is some importance in knowing what they think. If they are pretty much nobody to you, what does it matter, really? The majority of the time, people who spew repeated lies and rumors and tear a person down are sick individuals, personality-disordered losers who have nothing better to do than make themselves feel better by insulting others. And if they are creeps, what does it matter what they say? Leave them in the closet and let them amuse themselves without letting them get to you.

Get Perspective

Another thing your daughter needs to know is what kind of audience the sicko has. If no one is paying attention or they are laughing at him or her, the person can't do you much harm. One woman tweeted that she had less respect for me than for accused child killer Casey Anthony. She had tweeted more than 16,000 times and only had two followers! I don't think I have to worry that she is influencing too many people's opinions of me. Of course, if your daughter's bully actually is a popular girl at school, she may have more people willing to buy the girl's vicious stories about her. This is a tougher situation, but it is worth advising your daughter that her true friends know who she really is and they won't be swayed by the lies.

The other thing I would suggest your daughter analyze is how much impact her haters have on her. It can feel a lot worse than it really is. We may allow those words to seep into our souls and cause us to feel they are truly destroying us, but it is mostly in our own minds. I watch to see how much of an effect any of the nasty stuff being said is really having on my family, my friends, my work, and my income.

We often don't know if some gossip turned someone off about us (even if it was not at all true). We can't worry about all the stuff we can't control; sometimes gossip helps us and sometimes it hurts us. Hey, I have had people contact me and tell me that someone they couldn't stand—the person who raved on and on about how rotten I was—actually made them want to hire me! So you never know how things will work out.

How to Deal with Insults and Stupid Comments

If your daughter is going to be on the Internet, prepare her for these kinds of people showing up. In fact, she should be forewarned about the same types in school. Because two of my children are mixed race and one is black (white mom, Jamaican father, one adopted), I warned them early on that some insecure kid who needs someone to pick on will someday show up and say dumb things. I ran them through a bunch of possible comments and taunts they might hear: the N-word, "zebra," and "Why do you have a white mother?" Then I instructed them to not respond in an angry or negative way, to walk away, and to keep a sense of humor. We had a discussion about why kids might say these things: ignorance, repeating what their parents have said, wanting to be in with some other kids, or just because they are mean, rotten people. I told them to start with giving others the benefit of the doubt, because they just might not know better; you shouldn't cross anyone off the friend list too quickly. If they continue with slurs, raise your eyebrows, smile, shake your head, and walk away. It isn't worth it to continue wasting your time worrying about them or what they say.

I encouraged my kids to have a sense of humor. I gave them a couple of examples. Once when I was crossing the Canadian border (without my husband), and the border guard looked in the backseat of my car and asked, "Are those your children?" Some people might have gotten frosty about that question and come back with an angry retort. I responded differently. I looked back at the children and then, with a mock-horrified look at the guard, I said, "Oh, my God! I always thought they were!" He burst out laughing and shook his head, grinned, and waved me through. He knew I had gotten him.

Another time, when I was moving into my first apartment with my Jamaican husband, he was unloading down in the street and two Caucasian friends of ours were carrying stuff up to the fifth floor. A curious elderly neighbor who lived in the next apartment sidled in after my friends had carried in a bunch of boxes. She came over to me and said in a low conspiratorial voice, "I am so glad you're not black." I leaned over toward her and mimed Groucho Marx with his cigar and said, "You're only going to be half glad when you see my husband!"

The little lady turned out not to be so bad. She immediately said, "Oh, my, I didn't mean anything racist! I was worried about loud music!" I told her not to worry, I would make sure my husband kept his reggae music down to a dull roar with the thin walls those apartments had.

I understood her concerns. I had the same ones about my neighbors on the other side of my bedroom wall who drove *me* nuts on occasions with their thumping bass shaking the plaster off. She became a good friend, bringing us homemade baked goods and looking after us. So teach your children not to jump to conclusions too quickly.

Kids will also go after physical attributes: being overweight, having imperfect teeth or a bad complexion—any deformity or shortcoming in looks. My son has a scar on his face from a very bad bicycle accident when he was six. He had to have his eye socket rebuilt, and even though the plastic surgeon did a great job, my son still has a scar under his eye. Sure enough, kids went after him for it. I told him he was like Al Pacino in

Scarface; then I told him, "Okay, bad example—great movie, but please don't start running drugs for the Mob."

I could relate to my son. I also have a scar on my face that cuts down into my upper lip. I got the scar when I was twenty-three. The plastic surgeon repaired what he could. When I looked dejectedly in the mirror and saw that I was going to have a fairly noticeable scar on my face forever, he told me, "Don't worry! When you get old, that scar will blend right in with all the other lines above your lip." Thanks, Doc.

I did get questioned a lot about that scar when I was younger. People used to be so sweet. "Hey," they would say, pointing a finger at my mouth. "Where did you get that scar?" For a woman in her early twenties trying to look attractive, this was not what I wanted to hear. But I learned to roll with it. I would tell them I was jumped by a knife-wielding gang, and I managed to use my martial-arts techniques and escape with, luckily, only this one gash to the face. After they looked all impressed, I would tell them, "Nah, I got attacked by a psycho cat in Denmark." That was the truth. (And I have no idea why I have four of the dodgy little creatures in my house today.) In a way, the scar probably helped me move away from my thoughts of a modeling career and into a more practical mind-set about my future. It is rather ironic that later on I ended up doing so much television work in spite of that scar.

My son learned to handle the comments about his face

with humor and grace. Eventually, he grew to six feet and lifted weights, and the scar, which added a bit of dangerous mystery to his persona, is hardly what the ladies noticed.

A sense of humor can carry one through a lot of nastiness. One of my haters took to making mock tabloid "front pages" with pictures of me (bad ones), adding insults for headlines. Then he Photoshopped other pictures he found of me online. I actually started looking forward to seeing what he would come up with next; my favorite made me burst out laughing. This person had cleverly attached my head to a slug. I have made a gallery of these pictures in my office. They keep me humble and also remind me that you will always have enemies and people who try to take you down. I am still kicking and working, and I don't let them get to me.

If you prepare your daughter ahead of time for what might be coming her way, you will be surprised how much it will help. She will not be as shocked and distraught when it happens because she will have expected such behavior to be aimed at her one day. She will be better equipped to respond to it, and she will know she can come home and talk to you.

"Hey, Mom! You were right! You wouldn't believe what this girl called me today!"

If your daughter is ready for what is out there, she will be ahead of the game and better able to take it in stride.

Get Your Daughter to Take Control (or Do It for Her)

Now what should she do about the crap she will run into on her social-media sites and texting? First of all, teach her *she* is in control. There have been many news stories about a girl being brutally harassed on the Internet to the point where she commits suicide. I have to point out that the girl has some responsibility in this matter, as do her parents. What would you say to your daughter if she told you that every time she went to Mary's house, there was a group of horrible teens over there making fun of her and calling her every name in the book? You probably would say, *"Don't go over there!"* Is this rocket science?

And if your daughter keeps going over to Mary's house day after day and keeps coming home crying day after day, she has problems, and so do you, her parents, for allowing her to do that to herself. If someone keeps returning for abuse, there is a problem with the individual, not just with the abuser.

So while it may be said that this particular girl was driven to suicide by Internet harassment, there was something already amiss in the mind of the victim, perhaps very shaky self-respect or a problem she has not gotten help with, and that is why she kept going back for abuse and ended up killing herself over it. I am not saying the abusers aren't horrible people and aren't guilty of cruelty; they are. But anyone who gives herself over to be tormented has issues, and that is the part you and your daughter control; one can usually avoid being a victim if one chooses to.

So if your daughter is getting trashed on social media, you need to sit down and figure out why, how, and what she can do to solve the problem. Here are some ideas to help:

1. Get the problem in perspective. Again, not all rubbishing of someone is without merit. Check and see whether your daughter is the one instigating the problem. Suppose my daughter comes home and says some other girl punched her in the face. My first question would be, "Did you deserve it?" (Okay, maybe not my first, but it is in the queue). Again, I'm not saying the attacker is correct, but sometimes it is one's own child who starts something, throws out an insult or a bit of slander, and gets a reaction. In the old days, a parent might have said, "Well, darlin', you had it coming." Today there is a tendency to believe we are blaming the victim if we suggest such a thing, for there is "never a reason for someone to be victimized." I tend to disagree. It may be a crime to victimize someone, but sometimes there is a reason we can understand. It's still wrong, but the victim was not a total innocent. Find out whether your daughter is stirring the pot or not.

2. Encourage her to shut down avenues between her bullies and her. She does not have to have them as Facebook friends. She can "unfriend" them (that's where you can still see what they write if they have an open page, and they can see what you write if you have an open page, but they can't post on your page, nor can you on theirs) or she can block them (so they can't see her anywhere and she can't see them). Facebook allows your daughter to choose whom she wishes to communicate with. I would encourage her to only have actual friends as friends on Facebook, not just anyone from school or someone who appears out of nowhere and wants to "friend" her (which happens all the time on Facebook). I myself allow anyone to friend me on Facebook, but these are fans, and my Facebook pages are part of my business. Your daughter should be using her Friend page as a place to share her life with her friends—and only her friends. In my opinion, she should set up her page to be seen *only* by friends she has accepted, and not the whole world. This is safer in general; it keeps her out of the view of those who might like to friend her and then move in on her abusively as well as mean classmates and others in the community who might do the same.

3. Twitter is a bit of a different animal. People choose to

"follow" your daughter, and your daughter will choose whom she follows. The easiest part is your daughter's choice to follow. People follow for two reasons: they want to see what their friend (or someone they are a fan of) is doing or saying, or they want to stalk the person, keep track of her and her movements, and hurl abuse at her that they hope that person and everyone else will see. Once you have a Twitter name, people can put @ before your Twitter name (like "@ profilerpatb") and you will see it if you haven't blocked the person, and everyone else who puts your Twitter name in *will see it as well.* Put "profilerpatb" into your Twitter search and just look at the stuff people are saying about me. Some are responding to me, some are saying nice things about me, but some are going nuts (in all caps) making accusations, insulting and libeling me. If your daughter blocks people on Twitter, she cannot stop them from talking about her. But she won't see what they are saying, which is fine, in my opinion. But you have to encourage her to *not* look.

4. Speaking of not looking, this is by far the most important point. Anything that we are tempted to check out, especially those things that we know may pull us in, we should avoid. If you have a habitual problem with alcohol or chocolate, it probably isn't

wise to hang out in a bar or stand in front of the Godiva store. I can pretty much view disparaging comments and not have it bother me; in fact, I have gotten some pretty good ideas from my haters! *But* if your daughter hasn't matured to the level of having a thick skin and being able to laugh at insults, she should protect herself from deluges of comments that can destroy her self-image. Help her decide whom she should have communication with on the Internet social-media sites and how open her pages should be. If there are bullies out there harassing her and she is drawn like a moth to their burning epithets, you may have to take the helm of the computer and put a stop to her torturing herself.

If your daughter is on the weak side or suffers from ego issues, you need to be extra careful about having her put herself in the path of Internet bullying. You don't want to find her hanging in her closet because she couldn't stand waking up in the morning. The bullies won't be the only reason she committed suicide (parents sometimes refuse to admit their daughter had a problem prior to the harassment), but they may increase the bad feelings she has about herself or the world she lives in.

5. Chat rooms. As we noted earlier, these are places where like-minded people can have interesting dis-

cussions. The problem is your daughter won't know who those people are (unless it is a church- or school-connected chat room). She needs to know that she shouldn't go into *any* chat room that is just a place to hang out with no actual purpose, because these rooms are targeted by predators. If she chooses to go into a chat room that focuses on a hobby or an ideology, make sure she understands that any conversation she has should never veer toward personal information or sex. If it does, the person on the other end is very likely a predator of some sort; otherwise, he would be staying on topic. Your daughter should also realize that a stalker can string together information over a number of chats to actually identify who she is without necessarily knowing her whole name. For example:

Chat One: "What's your name?" "Angelique." (Unusual name, should be easy to find, maybe even on Facebook.)

Chat Two: "So are you in school?" "Yeah, high school, junior year." (Cool, I can find her through yearbook photos or school-related sites.)

Chat Three: "So do you ski?" "No, never have skied. Not a lot of snow in southern Florida! Ha ha!" (Okay, now I have her state.)

Chat Four: "Do you hang out at the beach?"

"Every chance. I love to swim." (So you are on the coast.)

Chat Five: "Are you a Buccaneers fan?" "Oh, big time. They are our team!" (Gotcha—Tampa girl named Angelique attending junior year at a Tampa high school.)

Chat Six: "Do you work after school?" "Yeah, I work at Five Guys." (See you tomorrow, Angelique.)

Does that not creep you out? This is how quickly it can be done. While it is true most sexual predators on the Internet don't waste their time with a girl unless she will talk about sex right away, there are those who just might be willing to wait or who might become obsessed with your daughter in some way and stalk her (more about that in the chapter on stalking). If the predator or stalker has a bit of patience, personal information can be had very quickly, because the girl forgets what she said in the last conversation; he can do a little investigating and pinpoint who and where she is without her even realizing it is happening. So encourage her to keep on topic, not give out even seemingly benign information, and never give her real first or last name in an open chat room.

Don't forget, it may be a good idea to not allow your daughter to use the Internet on a personal laptop in the privacy of her bedroom. Knowing that other people are in the room and that others will use the computer can keep her from going to a dangerous place on the Internet and talking about anything on Facebook that she would worry about her parents or siblings seeing.

The Internet opens up the world to your daughter. Be sure she travels to great places, not hellholes.

Finally, about that iPhone or other cell phone your daughter has: it is a privilege for her to have it, not a right. If you feel she is misusing it or allowing others to misuse her through it, take it away from her. You can always give her an emergency cell phone that allows her only to make phone calls, not text or have access to the Internet. She can live without having the same equipment other kids have, just as she might have to follow rules her parents have set up for her that her friends' parents haven't. She'll live—really, she will.

Dear Daughter,

I know you just love Facebook and all the other social-media stuff on the Internet. I know you love iPhones and texting and chatting with your friends online; all of this is fun. But you may run into a couple of problems. You might have bullies out there who will try to make you feel bad about yourself and drive you crazy (both at school and online). Don't let them beat up on you! The best way to do that is by doing that thing little kids do that makes one nuts: shutting their eyes, putting their hands over their ears, and loudly saying, "Blah! Blah! Blah! Blah!" This is actually a brilliant strategy! They can't hear what you are saying, they shut you out of their existence, and they mock you by making obnoxious noises.

You can do the same. Unfriend and block anyone who bugs you on your page. Do the same on Twitter. Keep your page private for just you and your real friends, and don't go to your enemies' pages to see what they have written about you and then respond. The fact that you are paying no attention to them makes you the winner. It is important to remember that you are not losing anything by cutting them off; you don't need people around you who are stabbing you in the back, do you? And remember, you don't need to be talking trash about anyone else either. If they block you, maybe you need to think twice about how you are behaving.

When you are on the Internet, beware of strange guys in

chat rooms. *You probably have heard there are a lot of sexual predators out there who are just waiting for you to give them a chance. How do you do that? By talking about yourself, your life, or about sex with a total stranger. If you are on a site that is about movies, and some guy starts asking you if you have a boyfriend, that is off topic. If he asks where you live, it is off topic. If he asks you what kind of sex you have had, it is really off topic. Sexual predators will try to get you to talk about sex with them, or they will try to figure out what your name is and where you live so they can find you. Tell strangers nothing—there is no reason to, and doing so is dangerous.*

Learn to control whom you talk to, and when. Don't let others push you around and say mean stuff to you. If you are having a problem with bullies or creepy guys on the Internet or in school, come talk to me and let's see if we can find a way to stop them.

Five

RISKY RELATIONSHIPS

E very girl wants to fall in love, have a boyfriend (or girlfriend), and be popular. Unfortunately, in a world where we rarely know our community members or our neighbors, and in an era in which families move quite often, the boys (and sometimes the girls) your daughter hooks up with may be psychopaths or individuals with borderline personality disorders who want to control your child more than love her. The relationship can become dangerous, even potentially fatal. Likewise, the adults in your daughter's life—you, your partner, your relatives, your stepchildren, teachers, coaches, bosses, and the fathers of the kids she babysits—can be a benefit or a nightmare, depending on what kind of people they are.

I couldn't actually tell you whether whom you are born to is the result of a lottery or of reincarnation to a specific life to develop yourself, whether it is the work of a higher power or just a crap shoot. What I want you to get from this is that *you* and *your mate* are the first risky relationships your daughter has.

Are You the Problem?

That's rather a slap in the face, isn't it?

Who are the most likely people to sexually assault and kill children? Those who are supposed to love them and care for them—their own parents and their own family members. Take, for example, Josef Fritzl of Austria. He imprisoned his own daughter, Elisabeth, in an underground bunker for twenty-four years, during which time he raped and physically abused her. Elisabeth's mom, Fritzl's wife and enabler, looked the other way. So the first thing we must think about when it comes to safety for our daughters is not whether *others* might harm them but that we ourselves might.

So let's be honest. Do you have a problem that can put your child in danger? Do you have a problem with drugs, alcohol, or anger? Are you so desperate to have romantic relationships and sex that you will bring people into the house who might harm your child? If you are the primary caregiver, do you have the support you need? Are you stuck at home without adult conversation, with screaming babies or unmanageable kids, and no one to help around the house or with child care? If you are a woman or a man caring for the children in the house and you are having a hard time getting through the day without a desire to leave your infant screaming while you hide in the bathroom, or you feel like picking your baby up and shaking it until it stops or slapping your teenage kids around just for opening their mouths, you need to get help. Don't try to pretend you can handle it; don't even think you *should* handle it, or that you are a failure if you don't. One of the biggest problems in Western society today, and increasingly around the world, is the loss of extended family living in the home and helping out.

When my daughter was born, I was living with my husband in California in a low-income (read: ghetto) apartment. We had one room, a bathroom, and a kitchen. We had little money. I was alone all day with an infant who seldom slept and was colicky (or so it seemed). I remember looking into my little daughter's deep brown eyes and telling her it was a good thing she was so cute or I might do something terrible to her. (I was joking, of course, but you can see she was making me pretty cranky.) I had no relatives around, and my husband was gone all day on job training. The one thing that actually made a huge difference in those difficult circumstances was that I lived in such a poor neighborhood that most of the women were home on welfare, and they were pretty good company! Almost like an extended family, they were women to commiserate with, chat with, distract me, and even take the baby out of my arms for a few minutes so I could go to the bathroom without carrying her in there with me. Often, when a baby, child, or teen is murdered by his or her own father or mother (or the stepparent, mother's boyfriend, or father's girlfriend) it is because the adult was home alone with him or her. With no one to keep an eye on behaviors getting out of control and no one to take the pressure off of the kid making one crazy, bad things can happen.

Admittedly, most parents, unless they have a personality disorder or are psychotic, are not going to end up killing their children. People without personality disorders might end up hiding in the bathroom for a while, spouting some bad language, or maybe spanking or slapping a child who has driven them over the edge. People *with* borderline personality disorder, narcissistic personality disorder, or psychopathy, however, may kill the child to eliminate the annoyance. If they are not alone with the child, they might not reach that level; or someone can intervene or distract them. They might not do it if someone is watching because they don't want to go to prison.

If you or anyone caring for your daughter finds his or her frustrations increasing day by day, it is important to take measures to alleviate the issues that are causing the problem, even if that means getting child care, putting the child with a relative temporarily, or getting the child into foster care. Hopefully, smaller measures can be taken that make a lot of difference in ensuring your children are safe and that your teen daughter is not the target of an out-of-control adult.

Okay, so let's assume you and your child's father are not Casey Anthony or the charming Mr. Fritzl. Neither of you is going to rape or harm your own daughter. Let's say you can keep a pretty decent temper around her, and you are not abusing her or making life so unpleasant she wants to run away. But let's assume that your daughter's mother or father is not living with the two of you in your home or that your daughter is living with the other parent. Here enters one of the most dangerous factors in a girl's life: the boyfriend, girlfriend, or stepparent.

The Danger of the Significant Other

What makes these people such a potential threat? The simple fact that they usually have less of a bond with your daughter than you have. Think about your nieces and nephews and the other children in the neighborhood. Yes, you may think they are great kids, but do you often think they are ever as cute as your own children? And do you find that other people's kids tend to be more annoying to you than your own? Do you sometimes feel a reduced level of positive emotions when deal-ing with them? Assuming you aren't one of those parents who has a severe psychological problem, it essentially works like this: your own children are awesome, your relatives' kids are sort of cute, and the neighbor kids are to be tolerated. Some people's kids even get the brat label, but rarely do you clas-sify your own in such a way. In fact, we can be so entranced by our own kids, we make other people sick! "Isn't Johnny so adorable going, 'Vroom! Vroom!' with his little truck?" (over and over and over on your leg while you are trying to eat). "Isn't little Beth a wonderful singer?" (as the six-year-old sings her tenth song off-key). And so it goes with stepparents and live-in boyfriends and girlfriends as well. They may say how much they love or like your daughter, but let's face it—prob-ably nowhere near as much as you do, if at all.

Along with this unfortunate reduced affection for your child, this lack of love between your daughter and the other person implanted in her life, is the ease with which negative feelings can surface when exacerbated by normal childish and obstinate behavior, whining, and outbursts like, "I want my *real* daddy!" or "I'm going to tell Mommy!" And when your daughter reaches her teen years, remarks like "You can't tell me what to do; you're *not* my father" can really set others off. Even parents who love their children sometimes find it hard to like their own teenagers; so how does a new live-in caretaker tolerate them? Often, not very well.

The younger your daughter is when a questionable character enters her life, the more risk there is that she may be sexually assaulted, physically abused, or murdered. The smaller she is, the more easily she can be victimized, and she won't be able to speak up. I worked on one profiling case in which a fourteen-month-old girl was sexually assaulted by her biological father who was caring her for the afternoon. Redness and mild abrasions in the vaginal area alerted the mother that something wasn't right. She took the baby to the doctor and filed a police report. Semen was found on the child. The father claimed the semen came from the bed sheets he laid the child down on and he "only" touched her vaginal area with his finger out of curiosity. He was convicted, and it turned out that he hadn't caused the child serious physical injury. Let's hope that Daddy won't be allowed near her for the rest of her life. At least she is safe for the present. But what would have happened if there had been no physical evidence of the assault? What if the child's mother had told herself her former husband wasn't that type of person? This little tyke would not have been able to tell Mommy what Daddy had done to her. The sexual assaults could have gone on for years.

Anyone, male or female, whom you bring into your house and leave alone with your daughter can abuse your child for months or years without you having a clue. Even if your daughter has emotional issues, you may attribute her acting-out behaviors and crying and fears as age-related or connected to some other events in her life. By the time you realize (if ever you do) what has really been going on, it may be too late to reverse the damage.

Along with committing sexual assaults, stepparents and live-in adults may physically or emotionally abuse children out of frustration, jealousy, irritation, or a lack of emotional connection with them. Even though your partner or lover knew kids "came with the deal," it doesn't mean he or she realized they were going to be so much trouble to live with or take up so much of your time. Jaycee Dugard, who was abducted at age eleven and held captive for years by Phillip Garrido, often speaks more negatively about her stepfather than she does of the man who stole her from her family, imprisoned her, and raped her. Why? Garrido paid more attention to Jaycee than her stepfather did, treated her as his "special" girl, bringing her kittens and things she wanted (even though he also ignored her requests many times).

Jaycee always felt her stepfather loved her little sister, his biological daughter, but didn't have much use for her. The bitterness she feels about this is very clear in her writing. She felt he belittled her, made her feel bad about herself, and wasn't there when she needed a father to protect and guide her.

Are all stepparents or significant others going to treat your daughter like Cinderella or worse? Of course not. But since there are always stories in the news of young girls and teens being harmed by the adults who have been brought into their lives, one has to be vigilant regarding this new person that *you* have invited into your life (most of the time it is the adult, not the children, who want the second adult to move in). You must make sure he or she is beneficial to your number one priority—and that is your children, not you. It is simply too bad if you are lonely or want sex or help with the household expenses; your duty is to your children first. Before you bring anyone into your daughter's life, be darned sure he or she isn't going to be detrimental in any way.

What Were You Thinking?

Some of these poor choices of boyfriend or girlfriend should be quite obvious; yet someone is always out there ignoring the obvious and making excuses for hooking up with clearly questionable individuals. For example, going online to a felon dating site (yes, there are many of them on the Internet) is truly fishing for bottom-feeders in a dirty pond. If you have children, there is no excuse for you to be scraping the bottom of the barrel for companionship. While it is true that one might have to kiss a few frogs before finding the right partner, there is no excuse for throwing down with hyenas that will eat your children for breakfast.

And, no, good-hearted men and women, dating criminals is *not* a Christian duty. This is not how you express your superhuman forgiveness and give them another chance in life. Criminals should not be "dating" anyone until they are out of prison, have finished with parole, have cleaned up their lives, and have proven themselves to be honest citizens who can be trusted in a relationship. Certainly, no one should be romancing a thug who is still doing time. If you want to help the incarcerated become good citizens, work with a program that requires them to change themselves and pay back their victims and society.

Over at the date-an-inmate site, you find a bunch of men with clean-cut looks, nice smiles, and proper clothes. These guys say something like this in their profile: "I am looking for a woman who understands the value of friendship. Height and weight are not important to me; it is what is inside that counts. I prefer a beautiful heart to a beautiful face. I have made mistakes in my life, and I don't expect you to be perfect. I have worked hard over the last ten years here to get my associate's degree, and I read a lot on spiritual matters and developing positive relationships. My hobbies are writing poetry, singing a cappella, and working out. My perfect date would be taking a romantic walk on the beach, building a bonfire, making my favorite shrimp kabob recipe for my lady, and just talking and getting to know each other really well."

Doesn't this guy sound pretty good? Why is this? I will tell you! He is a psychopath who knows how to con people. He is actually inside for armed robbery, weapons charges, kidnapping, and attempted murder. Is this a nice man?

Are you a man? If you are at the female section of the felon dating site, please know that she is pretty slick, as well. She will say, "I am in great shape (I can't overeat here) and I am looking for a man who is honest, hardworking, and loves fun. I like dogs, sports, and a good action movie. My idea of a great date is snuggling with my man on the couch and watching football with a nice cold brewski! I love to make my man happy, cook great comfort food, and keep a nice clean house for him." Not only is this woman a prostitute, but apparently she also is in for fraud, identity theft, selling drugs, and domestic abuse. Is this a nice woman?

If a felon does actually get out of prison, he might have someone he's been communicating with (sometimes for years) waiting at the gate to take him home. I am amazed at how often someone fell in love with the inmate and thought it was a good idea to bring the just-released ex-offender into the house with the children. What is she hanging her hat on? That the new parolee has truly seen the light and is a changed individual and that he loves her? Then the recently released prisoner moves into the house with the new lover and kids, and a few weeks or months later one of the teenage girls goes missing and is found raped and murdered behind the building where the felon got hired a few weeks earlier. Who could have seen that coming?

It may be true that someone out there has befriended someone in prison, eventually married that person, and they lived happily ever after with no crime and no domestic abuse. Lovely story! But such a happy scenario is so rare it's not fair to risk one's children on such a fairy-tale ending. If you want to cozy up to a felon, do it when there are no children in your life.

But you may ask, "What do I do if my child's father or mother *is* in prison?" My suggestion is to do everything you can legally to keep that person out of your child's life (and certainly no unsupervised visitations) until that person has truly proved to be safe for your kids to be around. Your spouse or significant other made a choice to break the law rather than taking care of his or her own child; that says a whole lot about that person's lack of character and priorities.

And what an important example you also set with your choice of significant other. Your daughter will learn from *you* how to select a mate, what to require in a mate, and what level of concern one should have in picking a person who will be around one's children. If you think it is no big deal to hook up with some drifter who can't stay employed, drinks too much, and lies around on your sofa all day watching television and eating up all your food, don't be real surprised when your daughter thinks the local pot dealer would make a good boyfriend.

Have Your Daughter's Back

Any other person you bring into your home or take your daughter to spend time with can land her in a world of hurt. Again, you are the gatekeeper. If three men showed up at the door and you knew that one of them was a drug dealer, one was a child abuser, and one was a predator, would you let them come in and spend time with your daughter? Obviously not. Yet if you don't really know people well enough, or you minimize their behaviors—*Well, I know he got in a little trouble with the law two years ago, but he has kept all his parole appointments*—you are playing with fire, and you might be letting exactly those kind of criminals into your home to mess with your daughter and ruin her life.

A great (but stomach-turning) example of two biological parents completely failing their children is the horrific murder of Aliahna Lemmon in 2012 in Ohio. This nine-year-old girl, who had a number of disabilities, had a mother and a father who didn't make her environment a safe place. Her father, after getting divorced from her mother, married a woman whose brother then sexually assaulted Aliahna when she was seven.

Aliahna's mother (who had custody of her and her two sisters) moved to a trailer park to take care of her physically declining father, a *convicted pedophile*. She asked Daddy if a young friend of his was "okay." Daddy said yes, and the woman had the man babysit for her girls in Daddy's trailer (he had since died). Then, after a while, she left the little girls alone with this man for an entire week because she had the flu. Sometime during the week, Aliahna went missing. Finally, they found her—parts of her—in the man's freezer: her head, her hands, and her feet. The man had a felony record and a history of violence and was a wanted man in another state. He had sexually harassed and stalked a thirteen-year-old relative as well, but somehow he wasn't considered a threat to Aliahna.

At least three people were unnecessarily brought into Aliahna's life. We can dissect all the mistakes made by the parents in allowing these men to have access to their daughter, or we can learn the lesson that we adults are the ones who need to keep questionable people away from our children; all the excuses in the world for why we didn't protect a child won't help us when our daughter is dead and gone.

That "Cool" Older Guy

As your daughter comes into her teen years, you do need to look out for a man who might try to be a "father figure" to her (especially if she doesn't have a father who is active in her life), an older man who can "teach her about life," "guide her," and make her feel special. It is not unheard of for this man to be a teacher, a coach, a father of a friend, someone she babysits for, or even a coworker of yours. Or maybe the friend of her brother in college or an older slick criminal about town. The 2009 movie *An Education* beautifully portrays how a sixteen-year-old girl can be taken under the spell of a man twice her age. Like the young woman in the movie, your daughter can be terribly excited to enter a more adult life and be wooed and romanced by someone with skill and money (at least more skill and money than Benny, the boy in her math class who works at the pet store).

Such a relationship can start seemingly innocently, the man simply reaching out to your daughter in a benign, interested, but not overtly sexual way. In the movie, the family actually approves of the man showing their daughter about town because he is of a status and level of wealth much higher than theirs. The daughter and her parents all became entranced by the "future possibilities," the glamorous unknown, which, compared to the mundane life lived at the moment in their home, seemed worth exploring.

Which girls does this kind of mature man pick for his little Lolita? Girls who seem adrift from their parents, lonely, in need of attention; dreamers with no clue of how to make their dreams come true. They lack parents who can guide them, they lack a strong social group that they can connect with; they simply are rather lost, and then suddenly they are found by a man who totally understands them and can change their world.

Mind you, the older man we see in films wooing the teenager may be quite handsome, brilliant (like a college professor), or rich. In reality, the older man who moves in on your daughter is unlikely to be quite that attractive and tempting, but your young daughter still may idolize him because of what he does for her emotions. Do not discount the possibility of your daughter having a relationship with a man whom you don't consider very appealing. Sometimes our inability to see what *she* would see in him keeps us from realizing what is going on right under our noses.

So your daughter's eleventh-grade English teacher, a bespectacled man who is a bit awkward for thirty-five, offers to let your daughter stop by his house, just around the corner from yours, to help her with her creative writing. You think he is kind of a wuss, a mama's boy; actually, he lives with his mother, so you think it will be safe for your daughter to go sit in the living room with him. You give her permission, and six months later, you discover that she has gotten pregnant by the man. You find out that her teacher was using romantic poetry to "enrich" her mind as he read the poet's passionate words of love, praising her mediocre writing as great enough to make her into an international journalist, and later when they have fallen "hopelessly" in love, he tells her that when he finishes his novel they will go off to Paris where age doesn't matter and get a little flat on the river Seine. What average girl (yes, your daughter probably is) might not fall for this delightful dream?

Of course, the reality is he can't write all that well, either, and his only published work is a short novel he self-published on Amazon and sold six copies of. He never had a book agent, and he is just a bland little weasel with no special talents at all, especially in the "dating females of his own age" department. Actually, no, I am wrong. He has one talent: being able to sucker a naïve little girl (picking on someone weaker and smaller) into thinking she had an amazing future with him. You find out she was pregnant only when she comes hysterically crying into your bedroom one night, confessing the whole sordid story, including how she had the abortion that her teacher-lover told her to get but that she was having nightmares about it. Now her teacher-lover has been ignoring her, and she doesn't know what to do.

You step in, you get the teacher fired (for "other" reasons, since the school doesn't want this to get out), and he moves five states away and gets another teaching job in a high school. He continues his predation; your humiliated and crushed daughter may take years to get her head wrapped around what happened to her and get her self-esteem back on track.

And it could be worse. She could end up a young, struggling single mom, she could get HIV, or she could end up dead in an alley when her married older lover decides he can't take the chance of his wife (who has the money) finding out he has been cheating on her.

Just to clarify: The lack of parents recognizing a wolf in sheep's clothing is the problem here. It *isn't* your daughter's role that I want to emphasize, because while you may think you have taught your daughter all the tricks that adults might pull on her, it is overreliance on your daughter's "smarts" that gets her taken advantage of. She may not be able to recognize a weasel; it is up to the parents to see him for what he is and say no to the entire thing.

So your daughter, who is only in high school or college, is more likely to be attracted to the man in the Italian suit with the Porsche who can take her to the Four Seasons restaurant in Manhattan and then jet off to the Bahamas with her for a bit of fun in the sun than the guy in the faded jeans driving a dented ancient Honda who can take her to Chipotle down the street and then jet off to the cement park with one tree to sit on a lopsided swing to talk a bit.

It is not my purpose to knock the simple life. Quite frankly, it is often the closer-to-home simple pleasures shared by good people who are hard workers that represent the best life choices in the long run. However, can you see how stars might be clouding your daughter's eyes when that gorgeous hunk in the Porsche rolls up to her? The nice boy with the simpler life is what she *already knows*. If she is looking forward to a fine companion, a good father for her children, stability, and good morals and ethics, she might see the boy next door or the young man at her church as exactly what she is dreaming of. But if she is thinking of excitement, glamour, adventure, fame, fortune—all those unlikely things that make up romance novels, movies, and television dramas—she is not going to be hopping in that decrepit Honda if the Porsche is anywhere around.

Dreams may be unrealistic, but they are exciting and alluring. Older men can offer far more in the way of a new lifestyle and experiences than a guy on her level. Older men know this too. Rich older men have no trouble getting girls young enough to be their daughters (or even granddaughters), because those men come with piles of expensively wrapped presents. If your daughter has big eyes for another kind of life, there might be an older man just waiting to take advantage of her.

Is it always wrong for your daughter to go with an older man (assuming she is eighteen or older)? Of course not. Sometimes it can be the best thing that ever happened to her if he really cares about her, *truly* cares about her, and isn't merely using her to fill his egotistical needs (like having someone to control or a trophy wife to show off). If she is over eighteen, she needs to look at his history. If he has a history of being with much younger women, she is just going to be one more car on his long train. If he is specifically trolling for young women, he has personality issues she shouldn't get trapped dealing with. But if he has a stable and honorable past and they happen to became acquainted, grow to like each other, and fall in love, he might be okay.

But how do you help your minor daughter (or your of-age daughter) not get swept away by older guys who are going to use and abuse her and dump her when they get bored or she gets too old for them?

"Rescue Me!"

Primarily, your daughter needs to have two things: self-respect and the ability for delayed gratification. Girls who fall for guys like this want attention and excitement, and they want it now. The reason they need this attention so much and want it now is that they don't know how to get positive attention and don't think they ever will. Remember Bella and her beloved Edward from *Twilight*? What is Bella's problem? First of all, she has very low self-esteem. She doesn't think she has much going for herself with looks or intelligence or hobbies (does the girl even have one hobby?). She has parents who seem to try hard, but her mother is sort of an old hippie—loving but goofy and childlike—and her father wants to be a good father, but he is distant and awkward with his teen daughter, whom he hasn't spent much time with in years.

Bella does get some attention from her classmates when she arrives in town, and there are boys who like her and want to date her. But think about those boys. What do they offer? Not much, in Bella's mind. They can't transform her into an amazing, beautiful, fascinating woman, nor can they offer anything all that exciting, just a night at the movies or the Dairy Queen and a bunch more years in rainy Washington. Even Jacob, closer to Bella's age than Edward is, will not transform her or move her to a different locale. She would have to continue to be just Bella and hang out with guys who bark a lot.

But, oh, then comes Edward, the much older (by a couple hundred years) man. He is very different from all the other boys (he sparkles, in fact). He is super-powerful and can save Bella from danger and fast-moving, heavy objects. He can pick her up and fly with her in his arms at miraculous speed. His family is far more educated than hers, and he has centuries of experience traveling the world. Also, bad vampires chase them about and clash and kill, and there is so much more excitement than Bella will ever see working at the local Walmart.

By the third installment of the Twilight series, Bella gets to marry Edward long before any of her friends head down that path. Then he flies her off to Rio, where he beds her with the excessive gusto of a vampire mating a human, and, apparently, in spite of his aggressive and very physical approach, he far exceeds the skills of any high-school boy in bed; Bella is glowing in the morning. Then those exciting experiences accelerate, and she gets pregnant and swells with a full-term fetus in just a few weeks and has a baby explode out of her and then— I don't know. The movie ends, and the fourth installment is not out at the time of this book's writing. I have read the book and already forgotten what comes next.

Bella wanted attention. She wanted to feel better about herself. She wanted to experience an immediate transformation rather than work her way over the next decade to achieve these things for herself. So she chose Edward over a human boy and even over Jacob, whom she would not have to become one of the living dead to be with.

Bella definitely got some of what she wanted. She got to feel special when Edward chose her. She got adventure. She got to move on quickly with her life. But like many stories of young women being manipulated and carried off by older men, there is unlikely to be a happy ending, regardless of what the author, Stephenie Meyer, might write. Bella died and became a vampire. She will drink blood for eternity, and Edward will grow sick of her as she becomes less of a novelty, less naïve, less dependent, less amazed by everything "Edward." He will eventually dump her and go find some other young thing to play with. She will forever roam the earth as a ghoul watching her parents and everyone she ever knew who isn't a vampire die. There is a bit of an argument about whether Jacob will die because he is a were-wolf, but I will not go into that. In theory, she can't get him back because Jacob is now pairing up with her daughter (okay, something came back to me from the book). Suffice it to say, Bella is going to be an unhappy old vampire lusting after some high-school teenager herself at some point in her long, long, long life. It is important to remember that the Twilight series is a fantasy, and fantasy allows the author to create any totally unlikely and improbable ending she wants. Real life is not so kind.

Your girl will likely be more summarily dumped with not nearly such exciting tales to tell. Most teens who take up with older men are just getting a slightly more experienced player from the neighborhood. It is one thing if you marry Tiger Woods and after it all falls apart you go out and buy a twelve-million-dollar house on the beach. Your daughter will probably not walk away with more than she came in with except for a baby or two and a world of hurt feelings. She might end up with a prison sentence if she becomes a Bonnie to some Clyde.

The Boyfriend

Now to perhaps one of the most important people you need to consider being a part of your daughter's life: her boyfriend.

There once was (and still is, in some cultures) a reason the family arranged a marriage and young women didn't date and pick their own marriage partners. A young girl was considered not to be wise enough and to be too easily swayed by falling in love (or lust) to think clearly. Even if a marriage wasn't arranged, the family carefully screened its daughter's beaus to limit her field of error.

Today we tend to scoff at such parental involvement in a girl's romantic interests, but it is not such a bad idea. When one considers the lifelong ramifications a sexual partnership engenders for both partners, their families, and their children, then whom a daughter (or son) dates and marries is not a matter to be taken as lightly as we take it in many societies today.

Let's start with an obvious parental "Hell, no!" to someone the daughter might hook up with. Even for highly liberal moms and dads who state that they believe in keeping out of the daughter's business and letting her make her own choices in romantic matters, there is a line (just like the line in another direction, where everyone has a price and says, "Hell, yes!"). Let's look at those, just so you can understand that we are all responsible to some extent for our daughters' choices.

1. "Mom, I am going to date Joran van der Sloot!" (the Aruban man suspected of killing Natalee Holloway and convicted of killing Stephany Flores of Peru, where he is incarcerated).

2. "Dad, I am going to date Uncle Rodney. Yeah, your brother, Rodney."

3. "Mom, I am going to date Warren Jeffs" (the cult leader convicted of forcing young girls into marriage and raping them).

4. "Dad, I am going to date that sixty-year-old, toothless, drug-addicted alcoholic man who stands on the corner next to the liquor store."

5. "Mom, I am going to date Sis's abusive ex-husband."

How likely is it you are going to hold your tongue in any of the above five scenarios?

Yes, they are outrageous, but these horrifying partners show that you probably do have a limit to thinking you should have no input on whom your daughter dates or marries. You do, but where will you draw the line at protecting, directing, and advising your daughter in these matters?

Hopefully, your handling of your daughter's dating life will start early, with good examples from your own life or your family's background or even history. Setting an example yourself with your own choices is the place to start. If your daughter sees and hears of women who made smart choices and enjoyed good relationships with men, she will have higher expectations. From there, it is wise to instill in your daughter a strong sense of self, a high level of confidence, and an ability to envision her future—*without* a man—and the goals she wants to achieve. Even a girl who looks forward to marriage and being a mother should want to be in control of becoming a successful adult and achieving her goals.

A young woman who sees a future ahead of her is more likely to be selective in relationships and not want to screw up her life by carelessly getting involved with someone too early or with someone too troublesome or too interfering. If your daughter plans to be a doctor or a missionary, she is not as likely to hook up with a drug-using musician who has two kids with two different women than she would if she has no goals and doesn't envision doing much more than making some money to get a piercing and a new pair of jeans. Your daughter with vision is not going to want to ruin everything she is working for over some guy who isn't worth it.

Is She Gaining a Boyfriend or Losing a Family?

Another important factor in your daughter's choosing someone to be with is her own relationship with her family. If she despises her parents and siblings, she not only won't care what they think about her beaus, she may date slimy guys on purpose just to cause her family pain, to mock them, to throw her behavior and choices in their faces to prove that they can't control her, or to prove how their neglect or abuse of her has made her lie down with dogs.

However, if your daughter is well-integrated into the family and shares the family's values and concerns, she is going to want her parents to like the guy she picks and the guy she picks to like them as well. She is going to want to have a bigger, happier family when her companion is included in the ranks; she is not going to want family members to shun her because they don't want her to come around with her man, nor will she want them to worry about her life with him.

If your daughter has a good relationship with you, she is also more likely to discuss relationships, present and future. She will come to you for advice. She will not sneak around behind your back in any major way. And if, like many teens, she does not tell you everything about her life, she will still be very aware that she might disappoint you, and she will think twice about what she is doing before she does it and will discontinue relationships she realizes are not healthy. This concern for her family allows her to be more receptive to wisdom about relationships and marriage and to look more carefully before she leaps.

Okay, so let's say your daughter has a healthy view of herself, her family, and her future. Is there nothing then to worry about? I wish I could say you are home free and your daughter will be just fine. However, there is one more area of great concern. Many fantastic young women with full lives to look forward to end up victimized by a boyfriend they thought was the right type of guy. Usually these fellows have a good look, walk, and talk, and their families appear to be stable and decent. Sometimes these young men are even stars of their school in sports, politics, or social groups. They are what we sometimes label sociopathic and what I call just well-educated, slick psychopaths or narcissists; they may not need to take revenge on society for its failure, to give them what they want, as serial killers do, but they don't like to lose in personal relationships. When your daughter hooks up with one of these, he thinks of her as the flashy car he desired; it is his until he is ready to unload it.

The Psychopathic Partner

This kind of relatively successful young person with a personality disorder often has parents who gave him everything and never let him suffer the consequences for anything he did wrong. He is their "perfect" boy, and they allow him to get away with all manner of poor behavior and bad attitude and fail to recognize his growing selfishness and lack of concern for anyone but himself. Because parents can live vicariously through their children, their son's successes are their successes, and as they push him to be a winner even at the cost of their own needs, his siblings' needs, and even his own good character, they may remain oblivious to what he is becoming.

When he misbehaves, or even breaks the law, they don't punish him. They cover for him and give him another chance; they don't want his momentary faux pas to ruin his rise to the top. He becomes a spoiled, self-centered creature with little empathy for anyone else and a massive sense of entitlement. But unlike less well-educated psychopaths, he is a smart kid who has been taught enough social skills and people-management skills to cover his personality disorder to some extent. A person of his own age may not see it at all, and a well-meaning adult who feels he or she has a responsibility to guide and encourage all children in all circumstances may acknowledge the boy has some problems but will never give up on him or think he can't be helped. Because of their kindly natures, these people tend to minimize warning behaviors and view cruel, selfish, and even criminal acts as childish reactions, immature mistakes, or adolescent angst. They think the children will grow out of these phases and eventually grow up to be perfectly fine adults.

But from my experience, what you see in a child of five is often what you see in a teen of fifteen and an adult of twenty-five, only with increasing physical and financial power at each stage.

Early signs of psychopathy are: *lack of empathy* for other

humans and animals (harming or neglecting them or just not caring about them); *lack of respect* for boundaries (stealing, going into others' spaces without permission, touching, pinching, and hurting others); *pathological lying* (about even unimportant stuff); *manipulation* (using others to get what he wants without respect to their feelings or needs); *sense of entitlement* (feeling he should get everything and without much effort); *irresponsibility* (carelessly shrugging aside things that he should take care of); and *lack of remorse* (never really feeling sorry about anything he does wrong). Lack of affect is also a trait; he doesn't respond emotionally the way a normal person would. He has a rather flat emotional landscape, and if you look into his eyes, you may get the feeling there is no one there. Anger is pretty much the only emotion he ever shows— and especially anger when he is not getting what he wants.

This list of psychopathic traits is something you should review with your daughter during a discussion of how she might take care in choosing friends or trusting adults in her life. She might find it fascinating, and you can find lots of examples on television and in crime books and articles. All serial killers exhibit these traits, and a good many other kinds of criminals such as murderers, rapists, child predators, and guys who kill their wives and girlfriends do as well. Both of you can learn how they behave by watching clips of them or listening to experts describe their behaviors (I do this almost every time I speak on television, and many of my clips describing these kinds of people are on YouTube on the Profiler Pat Brown channel). If you study these creeps with your daughter, she will learn to recognize these traits in any personality-disordered teens around her, and enough red flags will pop up to slow her down when it comes to going on dates with any of them.

It really is important to prep her before she ends up dating someone who exhibits some or all of these traits. If you then tell her you see these personality flaws, she may get defensive and say you are imagining things or exaggerating what you see. She may give excuses, minimize the behaviors, and close her eyes to warning signs. So teaching her early and getting her to be analytical (not judgmental) about those she is picking to be her friends, and more than friends, may help her steer herself away from trouble.

Would He Swim Shark-Infested Waters for Her or Push Her off the Dock into Them?

One of the most important things to drill into her head, especially if you are short on time or she doesn't pay enough attention to his warning behaviors, is this simple question: "Does he treat you with a lot of respect and care about what you need and want and what is best for you, or is it always about him, him, him, and making and keeping him happy?" It is not her job as a teenager to make his whole world what he wants while he crushes hers. Any young man who cares about your daughter should be concerned that she also is happy and doing well and moving positively toward the future. He should want what's best for her.

If the boyfriend uses and abuses her early in the relationship, it will only get worse. Teach your daughter that leopards do not change their spots; if he is abusive, it is not that he is just immature or having problems. Let her know she is not going to change him; his parents and teachers probably have been trying for years, and lacking success, have succumbed to excusing his behaviors. She is not going to have any luck, either, save him from himself, and turn him into a prince. If there is any hope for him, let him get himself together or get help from an adult, not her. Let him prove he is a healthy individual before she joins him. Even if he is popular and cute, if he has those terrible personality traits indicating possible psychopathy, he is not worth taking a risk with.

It is sad that an intelligent, attractive young woman with a lot to offer any man could end up with a psychopathic boyfriend. Why does she pick him? Often it truly is because of her giving nature, just like that of a social worker or teacher of troubled children. She may see the good in everyone and easily feel sorry for a guy with any kind of a struggle (and psychopaths are good at gaining sympathy, often for fabricated troubles). She may be initially drawn in by his smarts and popularity and then, when he starts not treating her quite right, she feels guilty about judging him and not giving him a chance to improve himself. Or she may feel already emotionally connected and find it difficult to bear the trauma of a breakup. So she hangs in and keeps smiling.

Often her friends are aware that something is not quite right. They may talk to her and suggest she get out of the relationship. They may even mention to you that something seems a bit off with the guy and they are worried. But she brushes all the concerns away with a smile. "No one is perfect," she rationalizes, thinking she is being a really good girlfriend by not tossing him for a few imperfections. And she might actually think she is his savior. There is a very sad song in the musical *Oliver* in which a prostitute who is beaten and abused by her pimp sings, "As long as he needs me." It gives me the shudders that this character feels she should sacrifice herself to a psychopath for "love." He ends up murdering her, which is not too much different from what can happen to teens in real life when they hook up with psychopaths. The psychopath may cause great harm to a girl—especially when she tries to leave.

No Boyfriend at All Is a Hundred Times Better Than a Psycho

An excellent example is the murder of Lauren Astley, a girl who dated the high school football star Nathaniel Fujita. They were a handsome couple. When she became concerned about his behaviors, she broke up with him. He tried to get her back into a relationship, but she declined. Then he asked her to come to his home to talk. She went, probably thinking she should be kind and fair and give him a chance for closure. Her body was found the next morning in a pond. She had been beaten and strangled, and her throat was cut from ear to ear.

What happened? Lauren probably thought she and her boyfriend would have a heart-to-heart talk, he would understand her issues, and they would part as friends. Nathaniel probably thought she would agree to be his girlfriend again but that if she didn't, she would never walk away from him again. He would get closure one way or the other.

After Lauren's parents spoke out on television about their daughter and her boyfriend and his family, I could see what happened. Lauren's parents were terribly forgiving and amazingly generous to the boy and his parents. On the other side, Nathanial's parents gave less. Lauren was similar to her parents—a very giving, possibly overly giving, girl. She was the perfect target for a controlling young man with a narcissistic or psychopathic personality. But she broke the cardinal rule—

mine, at least—which is to never, *ever* meet the ex alone if you can't trust him implicitly. I worked on a case where the wife thought her husband was bugging her phone and tracking her car, and she wanted to leave him. He convinced her to go on one last trip, a canoe trip in the wilderness, to see if their relationship had a chance. It was one last trip, all right. She drowned "accidentally" in three feet of water. After wrapping her body in trash bags and canoeing back down the river, he put her body in the trunk of his car and drove past large police stations until he came to a small, two-man police station. He was never charged with a crime, even though the police did not believe his story (the prosecutor didn't want to bother with a trial for out-of-towners because it was costly for the jurisdiction).

A romantic relationship is something that should be rare and special for your daughter and not something to be hurried into with any character who wants her. Too much can be made of dating, falling in love, and having a boyfriend at early ages. The biggest problem with all of this happening when your daughter is so young is that the person she falls in love with at age fifteen is not likely to be the one she wants to stay with forever. Someone is going to get hurt. And, yes, sometimes we have to survive a broken heart, but pushing the issue so early is not a great idea. Immature teens are trying to navigate uncharted and emotional waters before they have grown up, before they have an idea what they want out of life, and, most important, what they want in a partner. We have a hard enough time knowing what to look for in a partner as adults; it is much harder for teens.

With so many families moving so often these days, the chances that you know the family of your daughter's boyfriend are pretty low. You will have trouble evaluating the environment in which the boy grew up, and you won't know his history. It is always a good idea for your daughter to know a person's background before moving into a relationship. If you are going to allow dating before your daughter is eighteen, you need to work with her to establish rules for dating that will allow her to get to know the boy as a friend, and in a group setting or event. The family should get to know him as well. Old-fashioned, yes. Safer, yes.

If you and your daughter have a good relationship and she respects your opinion (which should be given not as a friend but as an adult and a parent with experience), you will have a better chance of influencing her choices of boys and relationships.

It's important that you get across to her that his needs should not outweigh hers. His wants should not outweigh hers. His behavior toward her should always be one of respect. He should also have respect for her family, her friends, other adults, and even waiters in restaurants. He should never lie. If she catches him lying, she should cut him off quickly. Liars are not good people. He should never abuse her. Abusers are not good people. She should understand it is not her job to save him from himself, and she won't be able to do so anyway. In fact, it is better for him to know she will not lower her standards for him. He will either rise to the occasion or go away. She should have those standards in place from the day she meets him, and that means her parents are going to have to instill them in her before they meet. If she is confused about her standards, a psychopath will make sure she has low ones.

Slowing her down in general, slowing down her dating life, and slowing down her relationship with a particular guy will help eliminate most of the troubled fellows. They won't have the patience to wait for her to give them what they want. That should narrow the field to more decent young men. And if you can slow her down, by the time she does date or choose a life partner, she will be wiser, more secure, and more knowledgeable about where she is headed and whom she wants to accompany her on the journey.

Dear Daughter,

I love you, and you are very special to me. I know you are growing up and have other people in your life, and I can only protect you so much. I will try to make sure everyone I bring around you treats you well and doesn't do anything abusive to you; if I blow it with anyone, please rush to me and tell me what that person is doing that makes you uncomfortable or that what he is doing or saying is just wrong. I will stand with you and see that we take the right actions.

Please be careful of older men (a few years older or a lot older), because they can be really good at suckering you into liking them. They have practice with younger girls and you haven't got practice with them. So they win, you lose. Remember, if they are hanging around younger girls, there is some creepy reason they are doing so; women their own age probably don't like them and have figured out their game. So they go for a young girl they can control. Don't be that girl!

Now, I know at some point you will want to meet the right guy and go off into the sunset together. We all love a romantic ending like that. Actually, it can be that way later in life when you are an adult, but not usually if you get into a serious relationship with a fifteen- or sixteen-year-old boy, or, even worse, an older guy who uses and abuses you and lies to you, or any guy who gets you pregnant and then vanishes. If you want to have a really great guy, you have to be patient and wait until you are old enough and he is old enough to make good choices. And if you want a great guy, you have to be a really great girl! Hey, what a concept, eh? And you have to have really high standards! Only very special guys are patient, and only the really decent ones will wait for a very special girl, be willing to get to know that girl, and treat her very, very well; the rest of the guys will go for the hoes and the stupid girls. Don't be one of those girls, either!

Take a bit of time before you date any guy; make sure he treats his family, your family, your friends, everyone, and especially you very well. Make sure he is someone you would encourage your little sister to date. If he doesn't care about how other people feel, if he uses people, if he is mean, if he lies, stay far away from him. If you are already dating him and he doesn't care about what you want or need and it is always all about him, you may be dating a self-centered jerk or, even worse, a psychopath. And he may hurt you if you don't do what he says. When you break up with him, he is going to be angry that you dumped him. He may try to lure you into meeting him in a quiet, isolated place: DON'T GO! Too often you hear of a girl meeting with her ex-boyfriend, thinking she is going to just give him closure—and he murders her. He thinks he is going to get her back, or else. He gets closure, all right. Please know that this can happen to you if you have a psycho boyfriend. If you are worried that you have gotten stuck with a boy who is mentally unstable, please come to me, because we need to figure out how to get you away from him without him going nuts about it.

Oh, one more thing. Don't ever think having a baby as a teen is a good thing. Having a child is one of the best things in life, but it sucks if you don't have someone to help you, you are broke, and all your life plans get ruined. Have a baby when that baby is your life plan and you have the partner and the money to experience the wonder of having the child and raising it together. Don't forget, also, that the baby has the right to have fabulous parents, not a couple of starving, screwed-up teenagers who don't know what they are doing. Right now, enjoy being a teen, get your education, and plan a great career! Don't let a guy (or a baby) screw everything up. Get the career, then the guy, and then the baby. If you do things in the right order, you will have a great life!

Six

. . . .

STALKERS

*S*ome girls attract stalkers. Usually these are the nicest girls, the sweetest and most naïve ones. If your daughter can be educated to understand that stalkers are out there and can learn how they behave, she may be able to avoid becoming a target. If, in spite of all this, she finds herself stalked, she needs to know how to get the stalker to go away before he physically harms her or destroys her life.

Where Are All These Stalkers Coming From?

Stalking has become an increasingly big problem in all cultures and at all levels of society. I am not sure what is causing people to become obsessed with one particular person, or why they find it so difficult to simply move on and find a new relationship. Or why, sometimes, does a man or a woman simply pick another person out of the crowd to obsess about? Why do these stalkers need to make the other person miserable, or terrify him or her? Why do they need to "win" by making the last move in the relationship? It is happening more and more in today's world: certain individuals feel the need to stalk and harass someone, just to get attention. It may be because more people are finding themselves disconnected from satisfying family and community relationships, and a stalking psychopathy is on the rise. Regardless of the reasons, you need to educate your daughter on stalkers and help keep her from becoming a stalking target.

Most stalkers won't go to the extent of killing the objects of their obsession, but they can make their lives miserable and cause them to have to constantly look over their shoulders. Then there are the worst-case scenarios, in which the stalker can feel happy by only "winning" the battle he is waging with his victim (even if she is unaware that there is a battle going on) by annihilating her: she must lose, and taking her life makes him feel victorious.

Becoming the target in a stalker's crosshairs can occur after a long-term relationship your daughter has had with the stalker, or she might have hardly given him the time of day. However, there are three qualities your daughter must project for the stalker to stalk her: he must think she is desirable, he must think she is attainable, and she must have turned him down (if only by ignoring him or otherwise not recognizing his existence).

Unless your daughter is a movie star or a pop singer, she is unlikely to be stalked by a demented fan who then pops up one day and shoots her dead simply so he can be the last one with her and get his picture next to hers in the newspaper. Your daughter will know who is stalking her, or she will at least know who he is if he suddenly attacks her. It is very unlikely that the stalker will be a total stranger (unless she has attracted him in a chat room on the Internet; then she will know of him even though she cannot identify him).

The Ex-boyfriend Stalker

So who will be stalking your daughter? The most likely candidate is the boyfriend she has broken up with. (And these days, it could be a girlfriend, but I will use the pronoun "he" for the rest of this chapter to make things simpler and to reflect the fact that a higher percentage of stalkers are male.) I have already discussed at length in Chapter Five just how she might be stuck in a relationship with a person with a personality disorder. Sometimes that angry psychopath will kill your daughter before she even realizes how enraged he is. But other times, the ex will begin a campaign of stalking your daughter with one intention: to prove that he is not to be "toyed with," that he is the one with the power, and that he is the one who will do the dumping, not she. She will either come back to him or else.

Of course, this thinking flies in the face of reality. She already *has* "toyed" with him and dumped him; she took control of the relationship, breaking it off of her own accord. But no matter. It is exactly this reality that he cannot accept, because it makes him feel like a loser. In life, we sometimes get screwed over. Sometimes we lose. Sometimes it is our fault, and at other times it is not. But that is not the way a psychopath sees things. He does not accept that he is a mere mortal and subject to the ordinary misfortunes of life. He must, in his own eyes, win. He may commit a mass murder (*that'll teach those "bullies" in my school who mistreated me or those girls who wouldn't date me or those workmates who don't like me*), or he may stalk in order to put himself in the driver's seat of a "relationship" he thinks he is in (even if she doesn't). To the stalker, your daughter has satisfied all the requirements of becoming his victim: she was desirable (he wanted her for a girlfriend), she was attainable (he got her), and then the "little bitch" screwed him over.

Let's say your daughter has broken off with "Mike." She expects he will just move on. Most times, yes, even abusers will sulk for a while but then move on and find another girl to abuse and control; he will find a new victim. Usually this is what happens, even with some fairly irritating or creepy guys. But that's not Mike.

Mike calls her again and again, trying to get her to change her mind. Your daughter tries to reason with him. It doesn't work. So she tries not answering the phone. He calls every fifteen minutes. Then he texts her. And tweets her. And posts on her Facebook page (if she hasn't blocked her social-networking sites). He drives past her house. He follows her. He shows up in places he has no reason to be, except that she is there.

He may just get really creepy, or he may get vengeful. He might start a hate campaign on social media or spread nasty rumors about her. He may get a new girlfriend and use her (if he can) to harass your daughter. He may key her car, kill her cat, or physically attack her. He may leave "presents" for her, like flowers in her locked car (how did he get in the car?), a dead mouse in her school locker, or dog poop in her lunch box. He may "gaslight" her. This means doing things that are designed to make her think she is going nuts, such as moving her stuff around (her books on her desk at school), tapping on her bedroom window at night, or erasing her name off a list she just added it to on a blackboard. He may try to scare off anyone who tries to date her. He may terrify her friends

Before I discuss what your daughter can do to prevent becoming a stalker's victim and what to do if she is one, let me describe the other kind of stalker she might become ensnared with.

The Wannabe Boyfriend

This is the wannabe who desires your daughter and *thinks* (if only in his own deluded mind) that she is attainable. Then she has the gall to show no interest in him, refuses to date him, or she goes out with him but their first date is their last date. What makes this guy pick a girl who is unlikely to become his girlfriend? Narcissism. Narcissism keeps him from looking in the mirror and being realistic about his options.

Basically, the wannabe-boyfriend stalker usually picks someone who is unlikely to choose him. He sets his sights far too high. Now I am not saying that an average Joe can't get a beautiful girl, a poor man can't get a rich girl, or a man who works with his hands won't stand a chance with a girl who is getting a master's degree. In fact, sometimes girls like a guy who is different from them, or he may have outstanding personality traits or incredible talents that override her issue with status, looks, or education. But the kind of guy I am talking about here isn't getting to know your daughter and seeing if she is reciprocating interest. I am talking about a creepy outsider who *decides* he is going to hook up with your cheerleader daughter, your honor-roll student, or your sweet church girl.

He asks her out. She says no. How dare she? And so he starts stalking her. He is either going to get her to go out with him or get her to notice him. It is even possible that he will decide to kill her so that he will get to "be" with her, to touch her (so to speak) just one time and be the *last* one to connect with her.

This kind of stalker displays a behavior somewhat similar to what psychologists call erotomania. *Erotomania* is defined as an emotional disorder in which a person has an unreciprocated and delusional romantic obsession with someone who has no interest in him or her. But this term is usually associated with a person who stalks someone who is famous or has an extremely high social status. He specifically focuses on someone he should know is totally unattainable, but he thinks that *if* he can attract that person, *if* he can get her to mention his name (even if it is in a restraining order or in the media), *if* he can terrify her enough to make sure she is thinking about him all the time, or *if* he can kill the unfortunate apple of his eye, then he will have retained a relationship with her for all time.

The guy who barely knows your daughter or has never even spoken to her but decides she should be his is quite like the stalker exhibiting erotomania; the only difference is that he actually thinks your daughter is much more attainable than some movie star living across the ocean and surrounded by bodyguards. So he desires her, thinks she should be readily available for a great guy like himself—and then she doesn't give him the time of day. He starts on his stalking mission, following the same kind of pattern as an ex-boyfriend stalker. He may stalk her silently and secretively so that she has no clue of his interest, until the day he asks her for a date or finally lets her know she has been rude to him and kills her.

She knows him but didn't know he was obsessed with her. This happened to Annie Le, a brilliant and beautiful medical student at Yale, just days before what was to have been her wedding day. She went into a basement science lab at one of the Yale facilities and never came back out. The case of this missing woman confused the detectives because they could see her go into the building on the security camera videotape, but she wasn't seen leaving. It made little sense until they found her body secreted in a wall in the basement near the lab. This sickening crime was committed by Raymond J. Clark, the man who cleaned the lab's mouse cages. Clark had had an obsession with Asian women since high school. I believe he thought Asian women would be easier to control than Caucasian women—if he could just get one of them. I don't think he was simply attracted to their looks or any unique features of Asian cultures. It is not uncommon for certain men seeking power and control to believe certain cultures will have women who are easier to handle than Caucasian or African-American females.

Annie Le was known to be a sweet and friendly young

woman. I doubt she was ever mean toward Clark, and most likely she was friendly in passing conversation or at least smiled at him or said hi when he said hi. What probably irked him was that she was enthusiastic toward her fiancé and never noticed how "desirable" *he* was. He may have decided she was snubbing him, not because she was already in love with someone else or that she simply didn't go for his looks or personality but because she wouldn't give him the time of day. She was going to be a doctor and he was just a lowly lab assistant. On the day he killed Annie, he finally got to have an "intimate" relationship with her, and she would never choose her fiancé over him again. She probably had no clue that such a minor brush-off would lead to her death.

All of this is about as creepy as it gets. What can your daughter do to prevent being stalked?

How to Dump a Dangerous Dude

Let's start with the situation that requires the most involvement on her part: getting into a relationship with a guy with a personality disorder. Again, most of this was discussed in the previous chapter, but I want to add a few things. The boyfriend stalker and your daughter will have a substantial history together. Many of us can remember how hurt, devastated, and angry we felt when we were dumped by a boyfriend, girlfriend, husband, or wife. The more time put into the relationship, the harder we tend to be hit. We have more at stake (all that time and effort), we have more memories, and we are more humiliated if they toss us after we were "such a happy couple" (even if we weren't).

Even emotionally healthy people may stalk an ex, if only from a distance (on Facebook, by Googling, or just driving by the ex's new residence on the way home from work). If healthy people have a hard time letting go and dealing with a blow to their self-esteem, a psychopath or severe narcissist is going to take the separation and loss much harder. So if your daughter is going to spend a huge amount of time with someone and end up in a full-blown relationship, she should know what she may be getting into. Once she is in, getting out may be very difficult.

A lot of girls rush into relationships, into sex in those relationships, and into boyfriend/girlfriend status far too quickly. If your daughter moves too fast, the boyfriend will get the point that she is pretty easily attainable and, worse, desirable—not because she is nice and pretty but because she accepts him so easily (meaning he doesn't have to put much effort into getting her and he doesn't have to wait very long to get what he wants). Psychopaths have little patience; they don't want to have to earn their way, and they tend to want instant gratification; long-term goals are not something they care about.

Essentially, if your girl is easy, it works for him. She was desirable and attainable or attainable and therefore desirable, and now he has her. He thinks she is "his" (his possession) and that she should remain that way until he doesn't desire her anymore. On the other end, getting out may be a slow nightmare unless it ends disastrously overnight. What your daughter needs to learn most is to slow down.

Since a psychopath wants to get what he wants quickly, he will have little patience to get to know your daughter in a group situation and remain friends before getting intimate. He will not want to wait two years for sex. She will become "undesirable" very quickly, and he will move on. She also will become unattainable to him, not because she is acting like she is better than he is or doesn't want him but because her morals or the parental rules make her unattainable (read: not to be quickly brought under his control and dominance). By slowing down, your daughter can weed out personality-disordered individuals who might become stalkers later.

Also, clue your daughter in on the previously mentioned psychopathic traits. These are red flags; spotting them, she can avoid even becoming friends or casually dating these creeps. One common trait is simply lack of respect for her wishes. If she feels like eating Chinese food and he says, "No, you don't," and takes her for pizza, he could care less what she thinks or needs. If she says, "Stop!" for any reason and he doesn't—for example, he is teasing, touching, being condescending, or behaving in any way that makes her uncomfortable—then he doesn't care what she thinks or needs. If she ends up in a relationship with a guy like this, she will find that if she later wants to break up, he isn't going to care about her wants or needs at that point, either. It is about him, him, him, and he will almost surely lack empathy toward her. The bottom line is, she should *never* get into a relationship with a person who does not value her or her needs.

But let's say your daughter starts hanging around with this guy and then realizes he is very controlling, abusive, clingy, and not at all empathetic—in other words, a psychopath or disordered-personality type. What should she do? Clearly, from what you have just read, you realize that if she dumps him, he could become very nasty. He might not retaliate, but she cannot predict this. She is going to roll the dice if she breaks up with him.

The best thing would be for her to become undesirable to him. No kidding! In other words, she should get him to run away from her, dump her, be repulsed by her, and embarrassed to be with her. Yes, this does take some acting skill, and not all girls have it in them, but if your daughter can do it, tell her to go for it. What makes her undesirable? Sometimes simple things like these:

1. Talk about herself nonstop. Show no interest in the guy and what he is doing. Blah, blah, blah, blah, blah.

Oh, and talk about girly things—nails, hair, fashion, gossip. Blah, blah, blah. This is the easiest and least dramatic way to run him off, and it can be done on the phone, with texts, and in person when they are alone. No one else has to be the wiser. Since he is a narcissist, he won't be able to stand all this talk that has no focus on him.

2. Be clingy. Really clingy. She can essentially be a bit of a stalker herself. Call him a lot. Tell him she wants to be with him all the time. Tell him she doesn't want him to see his friends, only her. Psychopaths do not like to be manipulated and told what to do. They do not like to be chained down. They lose power and want out.

3. Be unattractive. If he thinks your daughter is really cute, she can be less cute. No makeup, bad hair style, ugly clothes. If she turns herself into a frump, he will not want to be seen with her. This obviously is a bit more difficult to do because she will be seen by others, and often teens can't go for this; but if she can, at least when they are alone, it might encourage him to move on.

4. Be vulgar and/or act crazy. Spitting on the sidewalk has a pretty good effect! Suddenly laughing

nonstop for no good reason in the middle of lunch at McDonald's may make him squirm. Psychopathic guys tend to want the girl everyone else wants, not some freak show.

5. Be sad with him all the time. Sigh a lot. Be emotional. Essentially, be a bore and no fun at all.

Now, if your daughter can't get him to dump her or isn't able to encourage him to go away, then she does have to simply tell him she is ending it. She needs to do it in the least humiliating way possible (to him). She should *never* tell him it's over in a place where their conversation could be heard by people they know. But she should also not tell him in a private place where he could become aggressive toward her and hurt her. She should tell him in a public place, quietly and calmly. She should tell him she just can't handle being in a relationship right now, any relationship, because of school and family pressure, so she wants to put dating on hold until she is older and more independent (or finished with her degree). She can say she wants to put a relationship off until she is ready to get married (that will make him happier to have her go away). Then she should stick to her decision and never, *ever* be alone with him again (and avoid small groups with him as well). She should say nothing to her friends except the same thing she told him. This way he can save face. If he goes around telling people *he* dumped *her*, tell her not to respond, to just shrug her shoulders and not get into a discussion about it. Hopefully, he will fade away.

Be Her Bodyguard

However, if this guy is beyond creepy, you will need to protect her. The more big guys she can have around her, the better off she will be. Stalkers tend to be intimidated by other boys and men, especially large ones, and will slither away rather than get into a fight or confrontation with one. Do not think that having a girlfriend keeping her company is protecting her. Stalkers aren't worried about another girl and may hurt the friend to get to or back at your daughter. It isn't fair to put another young woman in danger to keep your daughter safe. It is *your* job, *your* responsibility, to keep her safe.

How long do you keep up bodyguard work? And do you have an entourage following her around everywhere? I really can't answer that because there is not a definite answer. You may just want to keep an eye on things for a few days or a couple of weeks to make sure the creep has really disappeared. You may have to be more vigilant if he seems to be continuing to lurk about. You could be overprotective for nothing. You may think you are being ridiculous, let your guard down, and find the creep in your house with a knife. Pay attention to the hair on the back of your neck. Be as aware as you can about what is going on around your daughter and react in a reasonable fashion. Most stalkers are not that energetic; sometimes simply ignoring them will work. It is the bizarre and obsessive ones who are of more concern. Be watchful about which kind you are dealing with, and then decide what to do.

Dealing with a Stalker

What do you do about the ex-boyfriend who won't let your daughter go or the weird creepy guy who decides he wants to "court" your daughter by being obnoxious, relentless, and scary? What general measures should your daughter take to get him to go away? First, she should stop all communication with him—and I mean *all* communication. She must never take his phone calls (change phone numbers if necessary), she must never answer a text, even to say, "Stop texting me!" because that answer is a communication and he will feel he has made meaningful contact with her. One word or sentence from her gives him hope of another contact. He thinks he has made progress! She cannot let him win at this game. As with a child who begs and begs for candy at the checkout counter, she can't tell him no ten times and give in on the eleventh. He then believes he can be the victor if he can just wear her down. He knows now that what may be necessary is to hang in and repeat his negative behavior *more* than ten times.

So your daughter shouldn't respond to any of his communications. No answering the phone or text, no answering a letter; she shouldn't even write "Return to sender" on a package she receives from him. He will then know she got it, thought about him, and wrote a message to him with her own little hand. Success again!

I once had a female stalker who had erotomania. It is not so uncommon for women with high profiles to have both lesbian stalkers who "love" them and heterosexual stalkers who want to be their "best friend." This one sent me DVDs and a variety of other gifts. What did I do? I watched the movies and passed the gifts on to those who might enjoy them, but I *did not* answer her. Eventually she stopped e-mailing me thirty times a day, and the gifts stopped coming.

Your daughter should stop all communication and do her best to avoid places the stalker might frequent. She might take alternative routes to school, to work, or to friends' houses so he won't see her drive by. If he should sit outside the house, staring at it from the street, go out and shoo him away (sometimes you only need to stride toward him or his vehicle), and then have your daughter go on her way. If he won't go away, call the police.

The Restraining Order

I know you are wondering about a restraining order. Should you get one? Will it work? Well, a restraining order won't stop a very determined stalker. It may make him angry, more sneaky, and clever, or it may make him more aggressive and dangerous. For a less determined stalker, it may keep him away. The most important part of a restraining order is that it does draw a line, which, if crossed, can result in police action and jail time. This can be a good thing if the breaking of the restraining order can be proven and the jail time is significant (and he doesn't just get a warning or a slap on the wrist). Check out the laws in your state and see how strong they are.

The bad thing about a restraining order is that your daughter is paying attention to him again. She is letting him know he scares her; he may imagine that she thinks about him day and night. He may be thrilled to get the piece of paper with her name and his name together on it. I tend not to recommend this route unless he really doesn't go away with the behavioral methods I have suggested or he is clearly violent or threatening violence. Regardless of whether you get a restraining order, remember it is only a piece of paper, not a bulletproof vest. He can shoot your daughter just as dead with an order or without one. Many women—if they'd survived, that is—would testify that a restraining order did nothing to stop their exes from gunning them down on the courthouse steps.

Honey Attracts More Flies—and Stalkers

Whether they are an ex-boyfriend, an acquaintance, or an unknown male aggressor, stalkers target young women who tend to be nice and sweet, not tough, streetwise, and savvy. There are a number of reasons for this. They feel it is easier to control a gentler girl. They feel less threatened by a docile personality. And they often test this by crossing boundaries, by moving into a girl's space and seeing how she reacts. If she is really nice in spite of his inappropriate moves, he knows he has his pigeon.

I remember an evening when I went to a bar with a girlfriend. We were both just barely twenty-one. A middle-age creep tried to sit next to me and flirt. I told him to move his butt to another table. He immediately shifted to the other side of the table where my friend was sitting and started chatting her up. She smiled sweetly and answered his questions. I kept throwing barbs across the table at him. He wouldn't look at me and kept closing in on my friend. He started touching her hand, her arm, and her shoulder, and she politely let him. I finally got fed up and told him in no uncertain terms to get the hell away from my friend or I would get the bouncer over. He finally moved on. As my friend and I were leaving, she said to me in the softest of kitten voices, "You know that man in the bar? He was kind of shitty." I burst out laughing because she had such a hard time being mean to anyone. Sadly, she ended up in a physically abusive marriage, which did not surprise me.

There is nothing wrong with your daughter being a kind, decent, and giving person. We should all want our daughters to be that way. But unless she is in an extremely protected environment (such as homeschooling and other well-controlled situations), it wouldn't hurt if your daughter understood that crossing her arms, cutting her eyes, and putting someone in his place with a bit of confidence isn't wrong; it is showing the boy or man that she respects herself and that she is not to be trifled with. Being a little tough doesn't mean she can't be friendly. I talk to just about everyone, everywhere, but if someone crosses the line with me, I will change my tune quite quickly. As soon as the potential stalker sees that a woman means business, he will go find an easier mark.

Back in the old days, a stalker would be hauled into an alley or behind a barn by a girl's brothers or father, where they would see to it she was never bothered again. In today's world, unless you are part of the Mob or a vicious street gang, you won't be able to take actions that are likely to be considered illegal. Help your daughter choose her friends and boyfriends wisely, keep her guard up for anyone not treating her with the utmost respect, and teach her to speak up and speak loudly when some guy violates her space. Stalking is a crime, but it is hard to prove legally and hard to stop legally. Better that your daughter understands how to keep from becoming a target and learns how to remove herself from the situation as quickly as she can if someone starts stalking her or she sees the warning signs of a stalker's personality.

Dear Daughter,

Do you know you don't have to be nice to everyone? You certainly don't have to be nice to those who aren't nice to you. If some guy is disrespecting you in any way, walk away, tell him to move on, don't give him the time of day. Once he shows any sign that he is less than nice, keep away from him. If it's too late, and you realize that the guy you're dating or the guy you call your boyfriend is acting creepy and controlling and you want to get away from him, remember, he isn't going to appreciate being dumped; he is going to feel humiliated that you "aren't that into him," that he isn't good enough for you, or that you are calling the shots in the relationship. If he is even close to being a psychopath or control freak, he may become very angry and hurt you if you try to dump him; he may start stalking you to get you back (and to make you miserable). He may enjoy driving you crazy, and he may eventually hurt you physically and may even try to kill you. It happens.

So be really careful. If you can, to end the relationship without problems, become the type of girl he doesn't want and is embarrassed to be seen with: whiny, clingy, always talking about yourself, blah-blah-blah, obnoxious, crude, loud, and less pretty. Then he can dump you and feel proud of himself. You will be free. If that doesn't work, let him down easy in a public place where no one can hear you tell him that you just can't handle a relationship right now with all the pressure of your family and school.

If you find that an ex-boyfriend is stalking you or notice some guy you hardly know following you around, come and talk to me right away. I have learned what to do with guys if they won't leave you alone. We will work together to get him to stop and go away. Don't try to figure it out on your own. Stalkers are pretty hard to get rid of and can be really dangerous, so we need to join forces and fight this battle together.

· ·

Seven

CHILD **PREDATORS,** **SERIAL RAPISTS,** AND **SERIAL KILLERS**

*T*his category is probably a parent's biggest fear. We can all imagine (and feel terrified at the thought of) our daughter not arriving home at the normal time and then having hours go by until the police come and take a missing-person report. Then days go by and suddenly her body is found in the nearby woods, or worse, years go by and we never find out what happened to her. I feel sick just thinking about it. Although some will say this is a very rare occurrence, one exaggerated by the media, I can tell you, as a criminal profiler, it is getting worse out there, and far too many young women are being abducted, raped, and murdered. However, not all girls are at equal risk, and some activities and behaviors will put them at greater risk than others. In this chapter, I will make clear what you need to do to ensure that your daughter is as safe as she can be (without locking her away in the attic), so you can worry a bit less. I will also discuss self-defense issues—what works and what is a waste of time and why some of these programs are even a bad idea.

How Many Serial Killers Are Out There?

The FBI has for years estimated the number of serial killers at large in the United States to be about fifty—one per state. You might think that this is not such a bad number, considering the millions of people in the country and only one serial killer at large among the masses of people in New York City or Chicago or Los Angeles. Or you may shudder, thinking there is some psychopathic fiend stalking your city and you don't know where he is or when he will strike next. Certainly, women in New York City were terrified to walk down the street when David Berkowitz, the Son of Sam killer, was on the loose. Residents of Washington, D.C., and Virginia were hiding behind their cars at the gas pumps, terrified that John Allen Muhammad and Lee Boyd Malvo, the Beltway Snipers, were going to drive by and pick them off. The Zodiac Killer and Ted Bundy raised fear levels in California, and the Green River Killer put people on edge in Washington State for decades.

Of course, you may be pretty relaxed about serial killers, not having heard of them in your region for years. Good news, right? I hate to inform you that there is a much higher chance of a serial killer roaming your area than you think. I estimate five serial killers are living among us in every large metropolitan area and that there are quite a number living in smaller communities throughout the country. But you don't hear about them. Why? Because the FBI refuses to label any sexual homicide (or nonsexual homicide) the work of a serial killer until it has linked three murders to the same guy. If the killer isn't leaving DNA at every scene or piling the bodies up in the same park, the police will rarely tell the community a serial killer is out there; they don't want the pressure they get from frightened citizens and an aggressive media. So even when a young teenage girl is found raped and murdered in the bushes, word does not go out that a serial killer is at large. Yes, a serial killer. If it isn't an intimate or domestic homicide with a rape thrown in as a staged element to throw the police off, only a sexual psychopath crosses the line to brutally rape, torture, and choke the life out of a schoolgirl. Even if this is the perpetrator's first sexual homicide, we can call him a serial killer because you can bet he will continue. On the other hand, it may be his sixth homicide over a number of states, but police agencies from the different jurisdictions never connected the dots (the victims were of various ages and different races, plus an assortment of weapons were used—none of which means the same guy couldn't have committed all the killings).

The other reason these homicides are sometimes not connected is the down time between murders and the fact that the killer may change locations. Unlike in the movies, serial killers may take months or years to strike again, and by the time they do, the next murder is two hundred miles away from the previous one. Only when the serial killer stays put and kills often does he make the newspapers and television new shows. When he gets himself a name—the Long Island Serial Killer, the Boston Strangler, the Grim Sleeper—then people realize a serial killer is out there in their city. Meanwhile, the other four nameless serial killers are moving in next door to us, working where we work, hanging out at the dance club, or coming over to our houses to do some handyman work.

I think you get what I am telling you. Anyone you or your daughter comes into contact with could be a serial killer. Any route your daughter takes walking home from school or to her friend's house could conceal a serial killer in hiding. Just because you haven't heard about a serial killer nearby doesn't mean he doesn't exist.

The Triangle of Victimization

Now that I have made you totally paranoid, I will tell you to not worry quite so much. Serial homicides are still a very rare crime, and it's likely that no one you know will become a victim of one. However, it never hurts to take reasonable precautions. Serial rapists are far more prevalent than serial killers, and you don't want your daughter to have to suffer through that crime, either. While your daughter does not have high odds of becoming a victim of a serial predator, you don't want to stick your head in the sand and say it won't happen to her. It only takes one evil human being and one young girl, plus an opportunity, for this heinous crime to happen. I call this the Triangle of Victimization. Most of you know the "fire triangle," don't you? You need three things—heat, fuel, and an oxidizing agent—to get a blaze going. If you don't have one of them, you won't have a fire. Likewise with the Triangle of Victimization. This triangle needs three things for a crime to happen: a predator, a victim, and an opportunity. If one part of the triangle is missing, your daughter lives another day.

Let's take a simple example: Your daughter walks home from high school every day by the same route. Every day of the school year, she has walked to and from school and arrived home safely. Clearly, a victim was presenting herself all the way to school and back, but either there was no sex predator trolling her route or he saw your daughter but there was always someone around when he did, so he never grabbed her.

But next year, on the first day of school, your daughter leaves the house fifteen minutes later than usual because she wants to look extra great for her first appearance of the year, and by the time she rounds the corner where there is a little group of trees, all the other kids are already at the school. As she arrives at that spot, it just happens that no cars are going by. The predator has a window of opportunity, maybe just everything fell into place for him at that moment of time, and he leaps out from behind a tree and drags your daughter away from view. The Triangle of Victimization is complete.

Girls and young women who end up in isolated places—if even for a minute—present the most likely scenarios in which they can get raped or murdered without being involved in high-risk activities like prostitution, hitchhiking, drinking, or doing drugs. Your daughter might simply be walking somewhere, going for a jog, hiking, or bird watching. These are activities your daughter *should* be able to do without fear. *Should* be able to. Unfortunately, serial predators purposely lurk in parks, near schools, and at shopping centers, waiting for the lone girl in the dark parking lot, the jogger huffing and puffing along at dusk when the other runners have already gotten back to their cars, and the girl who decides to take a shortcut through a wooded area on her way home from school.

The One Separated from the Herd

Should your daughter ever go to an isolated area alone? Probably not. I always jog during the day when other people are running around the lake with me. I avoid driving lonely highways through prairies at night. I don't even live alone. Of course, life would be very difficult if we never could walk to our cars after the store closes, so it is likely we will take some risks just to be able to breathe. It is useful, though, to at least be aware of what the risks are, and your daughter should know them as well. She should learn what risks are worth taking and when they are just plain stupid. Serving your country in the military or keeping your community safe as a police officer puts one at a higher level of risk for getting killed. But one may decide one is willing to take the risk. Working as a reporter in a war zone, flying, driving, and having a baby are all riskier than sitting in a chair and watching television (but then you might die of diabetes and high blood pressure from no exercise and too much snacking). Teach your daughter the power of making an informed decision rather than carelessly wandering around and putting herself in danger for no good reason.

A wise plan of action is to discuss with your daughter places she wants or needs to go and evaluate the risks she might encounter. Together you can pick the most suitable and safe options. A bus may be safer than walking, going in a group is always safer than being alone, and staying in well-lit areas with other people (the greatest deterrent to all serial predators) is preferable.

Self-Defense or Self-Delusion?

Next, evaluate whether your daughter can defend herself in various situations. Serial predators always pick the easy victim. Why should he go after a six-foot-tall girl who weighs 180 pounds, boxes and lifts weight, and looks like she is doing steroids when he can grab a five-foot-two, 115-pound cheerleader? The tiny girl is easier to subdue, her body is easier to drag, her pants are easier to get off, and she fits better in the trunk of his car than the Amazon girl. Serial predators are practical.

Fat girls are almost never targets. I always get in trouble when I say on television that the chubby college girl was most likely killed by her boyfriend and the little pumpkin-shaped eight-year-old by her stepfather. It is a fact that serial predators like slim, small girls, so being heavy actually lowers a girl's risk of being attacked by strangers.

And what about self-defense? Obviously, your teenage daughter shouldn't be packing heat or carrying a switchblade in her boot. If she is, I think her street toughness just might scare off the killers. Pepper spray can be useful if she uses it properly and there is no wind; the problem is, if she doesn't hit the button on time and spray in the right direction, she is probably going to get a fist in the face very quickly. Weapons *can* be useful, but it does take training to use a weapon correctly.

It would also take a lot of training in martial arts before they are any use to your daughter. Some classes, which crop up on college campuses, especially after there has been a serial-rape scare, supposedly teach self-defense skills in three hours or three evenings; believe me, *they do more harm than good*. I have taken these classes to see what they are about and compared them to the martial arts and boxing training I have taken over the years. These classes are truly scary. First, the instructor teaches your daughter how to throw a punch. Quite frankly, it is painful to watch the girls. Most of them never throw anything better than a girly punch, which has no power and sports a bent wrist (girls tend to bend them downward). She will get her hand broken if she makes contact with anything. The kicks the girls learn are wimpy and clumsy, and the girls won't execute them so well in high heels. Escape methods like twisting her arm in a specific way to break a hold doesn't work at all when the guy grabbing your ballerina daughter's wrist works as a ditch digger for a living (and outweighs her by fifty or eighty pounds).

If your daughter takes *ongoing* martial arts classes, learns to punch and kick hard and correctly, and practices sparring to the point where she is comfortable being in a fight with someone (and not afraid to take a punch herself), only then might self-defense skills be a deterrent. Maybe she can surprise her attacker with one solid punch to his nose and then run like hell. Maybe just looking fierce and putting up her dukes like a man will make a predator think twice. Knowing how to fight is certainly a good skill to have, but your daughter won't learn it in three to nine hours. She will only get enough false self-confidence to get herself in trouble: she will *think* she knows self-defense now, so she can walk down a dark street and take on ninjas; unfortunately, she will find herself facing a vicious and angry predator the size of Mike Tyson and she, the terrified little flyweight, will end up quickly annihilated.

When my two sons were eight years old, they asked me if they could walk to the park alone. I asked them, "Can your mother beat you up?" Even at that young age, they got the picture. I told them, "When you can beat *me* up, then you can walk alone." I am proud to say my twenty-eight-year-old muscled hunks now go anywhere they want without me.

There is nothing wrong with your daughter increasing her physical abilities and confidence, but lying to young women just to make them feel empowered is simply wrong; it's like losing a game on purpose to your child, making her think she is better than she is. One day she will come home crying her eyes out because she's learned she actually sucks at the game when Mommy and Daddy aren't letting her win. Allowing your teenage daughter to believe she can fight off a man twice her size could cause her to lose her life, not just get her feelings hurt. The more realistic your daughter is about herself, her skills, and her safety, the more confident and accepting she will be of the decisions to be made as she grows up.

How Your Daughter Should Fight Back

What, then, should your daughter do if someone starts coming after her on the street or in a parking lot, grabs her and drags her into the bushes, or tries to pull her into a car? First, don't tell her to scream, "Fire!" This concept is seriously stupid; I have no idea why people keep giving this ridiculous advice. Supposedly we care more about something burning up than someone being killed. I can see the reason for it inside a building, but elsewhere it doesn't exactly make sense. I can't see that I would freak if someone yelled "Fire!" while I was out taking a walk. I would probably look around, and if I didn't see smoke or flames, I would think someone was telling his friend to shoot his pellet gun.

Yelling "Police!" isn't too good either, because in some areas, one could think someone is shouting out a warning to his friends to halt the drug deal or not to boost that car right now.

"Rape!" would seem clearer, but we don't expect to hear that, and we likely will stand around stupidly while the rapist hits the woman over the head. And then when we don't hear anyone shouting again, we'll assume we must have imagined it or someone was clowning around.

I like a shout that tells the person who hears it what to do: "HELP! HELP! CALL THE POLICE!" Don't tell your daughter to only yell "HELP!" because a good portion of our society would be too chicken to go assist her, so "HELP! HELP! CALL THE POLICE!" gives the repeated plea to be saved and tells whoever hears to get law enforcement to the location. If your daughter gets lucky, the Good Samaritan will call the police on his or her cell phone while running toward the crime scene. If your daughter isn't unconscious after yelling that and can get anything else out, it might be nice of her to warn the approaching rescuer with something like "HELP! HE'S GOT A GUN!" or "HELP! HE'S GOT A KNIFE!" The approaching helper knows what he is walking into, and that extra information will make sure he calls the police. If he has that information, he might bring his own gun along, or he might grab a big stick or quickly gather a few other people to come and help. If she gets that extra information out and still is able to yell, she should go back to "HELP! HELP! CALL THE POLICE!" She shouldn't stop until she is rescued or the attacker shuts her up. Even if he gets to her and knocks her out, every time she yells for help before she is knocked unconscious is a time that her words might catch someone's attention.

A helpful tool for your daughter to carry is a portable self-defense, security-alarm siren. It has an ultra-loud, torturous, 120-plus-decibel, ear-piercing sound when the pin is pulled, and it won't stop until someone puts it back in (she can pull it apart and toss the two pieces in opposite directions). This alarm is legal, can be carried on planes, and is very effective. While she doesn't want to do something to piss off the predator, like slap him or stab him (ineffectively) in the arm with a pencil—things that won't make him physically uncomfortable but only make him mad—she *does* want to do something that tortures him in a way that makes him want to run off, giving up bothering your daughter. Also, he is not going to want to be raping someone while an alarm is alerting others in the area that something is wrong; he isn't stupid. Ear pain and the possibility of the police showing up will encourage him to go away and try his rape another day. Handheld security sirens can be found at stores and online companies that sell self-defense equipment.

Okay, let's say no one comes to rescue your daughter, she doesn't have an alarm, and she knows the rapist or serial killer is about to attack her. Or a car has pulled over and the predator has a grip on her arm and is pulling her into the vehicle. Should she let him know she will cooperate and do whatever he wants? Will complying allow him to feel powerful, commit his crime, and then let her go? Hell, no, and no, and no. I say your daughter should fight like an insane person, go absolutely as ballistic as possible on him: stab her nails into his eyes, do an Iron Mike and bite his ear off, kick him in the groin, and call him every name in the book, shrieking as loud as she possibly can. Her chances of survival are actually higher this way than if she gives in meekly, and she may not even get raped.

Run, Fight, Run, Fight, Run

I am not saying that in every situation, with every serial predator, fighting is better than giving in, but I can tell you that a serial predator is more likely to let your daughter go if she is a pain in the neck than if she isn't. This is especially true if there is a possibility of the attack being longer and louder than he wants, drawing attention and possible arrest. Also, these criminals are well aware that having marks left all over their bodies is a good way to become a top suspect in an investigation and to make their wives question what they were up to when they said they were just going to the store for some butter. Predators don't want to get caught; they want to keep on being predators. It is easier to let a difficult victim go and get a more compliant one at another time.

It is very important to understand that your daughter cannot reason with a psychopathic predator. She cannot make him feel sorry for her. She cannot make him feel like she cares about him by saying a prayer. Psychopaths hate people, and they specifically despise their victims. All they want is to have total control over the victim, and even when they do, even when the victim is following every order, they find it amusing to choke her to death and then play with her corpse. Don't try to humanize a sexual predator; think of him as an alien, cold-blooded monster who will kill in the blink of an eye. Run, fight, fight, and run.

Your daughter should never let herself be pulled into a vehicle, even at gunpoint. She is better off risking being shot (and maybe surviving the wound) than going with the predator to be raped, tortured, and, usually, killed. Most girls who are taken away in cars and vans are never seen alive again. Also, guys who attack females on bike paths, in parking lots, behind schools, and behind buildings tend to be anger-retaliatory serial rapists and killers. When something goes wrong in their lives—they lose their jobs or a girlfriend dumps them—they want to get back at society and do something horrific and power enhancing. These kinds of predators may be brutal, but they usually are relatively quick about it. They may kill their victims, but it is over in a matter of minutes. Your daughter will have only seconds to fight back and make a run for it.

The kind of predator who takes a girl away in a vehicle tends to have more elaborate plans than the guy who jumps out from behind the bush. He may have a rape kit with him: rope, duct tape, pliers, gags—all kinds of unpleasant items. He may take your daughter to an out-of-the-way place and rape and torture her for hours and then kill her. Or he may take her home to a dungeon he has built in the basement of his house and rape and torture her for days or weeks before dispatching her. These are sexually sadistic predators, and the girl or young woman who falls into their hands is living a real-life horror film, too terrible for most of us to dare to imagine, especially with our own daughter's image in our minds.

Never Get in a Car

So no—your daughter should never allow herself to be pulled into a car. She should claw, kick, hang on to the outside, smash windows, try to punch him in the head, yank the steering wheel, pull out the keys, open the door, and jump. Anything but be driven off in that vehicle.

If she can break free, she should run like the wind, screaming her head off, toward wherever people might be. She should go toward any light, any sound, any house, any barking dog. She should run into the street, waving her arms, even if she risks getting hit. The predator might at that point just decide to take off and disappear.

Never Give Up

If for any reason your daughter ends up a captive, only then should she be submissive. At that point, he has total control and is not worried about anyone showing up. The longer she survives, the more opportunity she has to escape. She should watch and observe everything, looking for any opportunity to escape or to incapacitate her captor (braining him over the head, shooting him with his own gun) and then free herself. She might even be able to make a phone call when he is asleep. Her chances of survival aren't good, but she should never give up, because her chance to escape might be just around the corner.

Street Smarts

Your daughter may never be attacked, but when she is out in public, she should be aware that there are ways to minimize her chances of being assaulted. If she is walking down a deserted and dark city or suburban street, she should walk in the road, even if there's a sidewalk, and toward the middle if there is no traffic; it is easier for a predator to grab her if she walks along the very edge of the street or on the sidewalk near bushes and parked cars and alleys. If she walks down the middle of the street, the predator has to actually walk out into the street and drag her back to the side. This is a lot more work. Also, your daughter is more visible in the middle of the street than in the shadows of trees or buildings. Someone looking out a window will see the middle of the street more easily than an area directly below. If your daughter is walking down one side of the street and sees someone coming toward her, she should cut diagonally across the street, away from him, traversing the middle of the street.

Your daughter shouldn't stop and talk to strangers, but she also should not refuse a polite greeting; she should *not* avoid looking at him. This shows weakness and fear. She can give a quick "Hey, what's up?" or a simple "I'm good" to a "How are you doing?" greeting. She should not, however, appear smiley and friendly like she really does want to hang out with him. She should speak dryly, look over at him with an "I got my eye on you, buddy" look and keep moving, confidently and not too fast. A sociable but tough street-girl attitude shows the possible predator she will not be an easy victim and she will fight back. Keeping an eye on the man, even to the point of looking back over her shoulder while walking, shows him she is making sure he isn't going to sneak up on her and whack her on the back of the head (and it also prevents him from actually doing so). If you are out with your daughter on a dark street sometime, make yourself an example of defensive walking.

If your daughter is walking in an area where she passes homeless men or druggies hanging out, tell her not to stop, but to flash a friendly smile, say, "Hi," and keep on walking. If someone tries to grab her, these fellows may well come to her rescue because they feel like they know her; she is their friend because she was nice to them (even if only in passing).

A word about parking lots. They are scary places, especially when your car is one of the last ones in the lot and it is far from the light pole. What should your daughter do if she finds herself leaving a store or school and having to walk to her car alone in the dark? First, she should do a scan of the lot; if she sees someone out there, she should go back inside and stay with people rather than risk walking right up to a killer. A few patient minutes can save her life.

When all is clear, and she thinks she can walk to her car without anyone catching up with her, she should then proceed. She doesn't have to worry about anyone lying under her car. Who does that? Who wants to lie uncomfortably for God knows how long, waiting for the driver to show up? This doesn't happen; it's an urban myth that paints a lurid but highly unlikely picture. But she should lock her car whenever she leaves it and glance in the backseat before she gets in.

Security Guards Aren't Necessarily Secure

Should she have a security guard walk her to the car? This is a question I often get asked. Unless the guard is a woman, my answer is *no*. Did you know that a serial killer's number one most likely job is security guard? Serial killers love power and control and uniforms, and they usually can't pass the psych test to get into the police department. So they get a job in security, which sometimes even comes with a useful company-issued firearm to hold to the heads of their victims.

Security guard jobs are very easy to get; every other business, mall, parking lot, hospital, and office building needs security guards. Most of the time they are unarmed and are just there to provide a watchful eye, keep vandals and thieves away, and show a uniformed presence on the property to deter criminal activity. However, because there are so many positions in the field and because the pay generally sucks, the basic requirements for low-level security jobs are (1) the ability to breathe and (2) the ability to show up for work. Consequently, personality-disordered types or serial killers can get these jobs without much of a résumé, even if they got fired from their last three jobs. Heck, one serial-killer suspect I know held half a dozen jobs in security, two of them in armed security, in spite of the fact that he got an early discharge from the military because of a psychiatric disorder and had once been caught with a machete in his vehicle on a college campus! Would you want that guy walking your daughter to her car?

Most security guards aren't serial killers. Most bouncers (another popular serial-killer job) aren't serial killers. Most handymen—another fairly popular serial-killer job—aren't serial killers. But you don't want your daughter finding out which one is.

Is Your Home Safe?

We've gone over the normal activities and movements of a teen as she goes about her life outside her home, but what about safety *in* her home? Some serial predators case homes to see where there are vulnerable females they can attack or abduct. Again, safety is strongest in groups. If a serial killer is watching your house and he sees three male adults, two female adults, two teens (one girl and one boy), and a German shepherd, he is going to keep driving down the street. He will stop when he finds the house with the single mom or dad and a teenage daughter and one cat. He will sit and observe. He soon notices the mom comes home from work at 6:00 PM, but the sixteen-year-old daughter is there at 4:00 PM. He has a two-hour window to do his thing.

How does he get into the house? He probably knocks. Your daughter opens the door. "Oh, no!" you say, "my daughter would never open the door to strangers." Yeah, well, I hate to tell you how often parents say that and it turns out not to be so. There is some odd human curiosity that drives us to want to know who is on the other side of the door. So we open it with hardly a thought. Or your daughter might have told her girlfriend to come over, and when the predator knocks, she thinks he's Amy. She opens the door, a killer comes in, and he shuts the door behind him.

The psychopath on the other side of the door might wear a police uniform he stole or a UPS uniform he bought at the Goodwill store. Your daughter will open the door because she thinks she should. Or the predator may actually *be* a delivery-man, since these can also be easy jobs to get. The predator could be on his first day of his new job when he knocks and finds your daughter at home alone.

His next delivery may be an hour late.

There are other ways sexual predators can get into your house. They may come as handymen and, while working inside, use the bathroom, then unlock the window for later entry. Think about the last time you had workmen at your house; when they left at the end of the day, did you check all the windows to see if any had been unlocked? Probably not.

Keep in mind, your daughter doesn't have to be home alone to get attacked. While parents are sleeping on one side of the house, or even in the next bedroom, a serial killer with cat-burglar skills can slip unheard into a girl's bedroom. A little duct tape over her mouth and around her hands and feet, and in the morning, you wonder why your daughter hasn't gotten up for breakfast. The first serial killer ever to have his murders linked through DNA, Timothy Spencer, did just that in Richmond, Virginia, in one of his crimes. The girl's parents, sleeping just across the hall, found her dead in the morning, her body hidden underneath the covers.

So think about doors and windows. Open doors and open windows invite trouble. So does answering a knock when no one else is in the house. Check your house and think about how to secure those points of entry. Consider how enticing your house is to a predator looking for an easy mark. Stand at the edge of your lawn, gaze at your home, and ask yourself whether your house has a WELCOME, KILLER sign on it. Then make it less inviting. Share your home with more people, get a big dog, or, if you don't want one, maybe add a big dog bowl or a cute rottweiller statue. Other possibilities: an NRA sticker on the door, bright lights, or a video camera obviously monitoring the house—anything that says to the predator that this place is not worth your effort.

High-Risk Behavior

Police tend to divide victim behavior into low-risk and high-risk categories. For example, a young nun living in a cloistered religious community who leaves the premises only in a group of ten other nuns would be considered an extraordinarily low-risk individual. Very little she does would put her in a situation where she would find herself alone and at the mercy of a serial killer.

On the other end of the scale is the prostitute who works the streets alone. All things being equal, she will get in any car and ride off with any man, as long as he isn't waving a knife at her when she opens the passenger door. She is willing to go to a deserted location for the purposes of a sexual act with a complete stranger. A prostitute's chance of getting murdered by a serial killer is pretty high, even considering how rare this crime is.

Any behavior that puts your daughter alone with a questionable character increases her chances of being the victim of a sexual predator. Walking or jogging in isolated places increases her risks. Going to clubs and getting drunk and walking off with the bouncer or some guy she just met increases her risk. Doing drugs in a crack house increases her risk. Becoming homeless and sleeping on the street increases her risk. Even getting stupid for one moment in time can increase her risk.

There once was a girl who, after having a fight with her boyfriend, left their apartment in a huff. While she was out wandering around, she decided she might as well check a few places to see if there were any jobs available she might apply for. She walked into the local bowling alley and talked with the manager. She filled out an employment form and they chatted. He was cute and sweet, and he asked if she wanted to hang out and go smoke a joint when he went on break. She was in a bad mood, so she said yes.

He directed her to a door that led into an unused area of the building. He said he would slip in through the back and let her in; he didn't want the other employees to see him sneaking out with her. She followed his directions. He let her into the other part of the building, and they sat down just inside on the floor and smoked the weed and chatted. Not so abnormal for a couple of young people (she was just twenty-two and he was about thirty).

After twenty minutes, his break was over, and he told her he had to get back to work. He instructed her to follow him out the back so he wouldn't get caught "playing hooky" with her. He indicated they would need to go down some stairs into the basement and then out the back way.

Suddenly, the girl felt something was wrong. She felt the "gift of fear," as security specialist Gavin de Becker would call it. (Becker is the author of the book of that name in which he advises women how to pay attention to their gut feelings about danger.) She told the man she wouldn't go out that way, and she stood next to the glass door at the front.

He looked at her with dead eyes and said, "You think I am going to kill you, don't you?"

She looked straight back at him and said, "Yes, I do."

He let her out the front door. Whether he did this because he knew she would put up one hell of a fight or because he admired her for being so direct with him, we will never know.

One thing I do know: I am happy to be alive, because that dumb girl who went off to smoke dope with a stranger was me.

Teach your daughter that any time she drinks or does drugs or throws caution to the wind, she ceases to think clearly and sets herself up as a possible victim of some psychopath she has allowed herself to end up alone with. Risky behavior isn't called risky for no reason. It can be a matter of life or death.

Dear Daughter,

I bet you have heard a lot about teenagers getting attacked by serial rapists and murdered by serial killers; those stories are always making the headlines in the papers and on television news. True-crime books are almost always about serial killers, and the victims are usually young women. You may worry how safe your neighborhood is, how dangerous it is to go jogging, to walk to school or to your car in the parking lot, or even to be at home alone. I can tell you that most of the time nothing will happen, but you never know if you and that one horrible serial predator might end up at the same location at the same time.

There are some easy ways to keep safe, though. The most important way to keep from being a predator's victim is having witnesses, witnesses, witnesses. Walk with friends, not all alone down a lonely country road. Don't jog by yourself along wooded paths, and don't have the bouncer at a nightclub walk you to your car and end up alone with him in the dark. Be aware of your surroundings at all times; don't walk or jog with earphones stuck in your ears and your eyes gazing blankly ahead. You won't even see someone come near you with a rock in his hand.

What should you do if you are grabbed by a man while walk-ing? Scream, "HELP! HELP! CALL THE POLICE!" Scream it over and over as long as you can. Someone might hear you and rescue you. Meanwhile, fight like crazy, scratching and biting. He might give up and go away. If someone grabs you and tries to pull you into a car, fight like a wildcat. He is not going to drive you home after he rapes you. Always assume a sexual predator is going to do you in, and fight as hard as you can; it is your best chance of survival. If you are abducted, break away if you can and run like the wind toward people, lights, cars, barking dogs—anyplace you might get help.

If you are at home alone, don't open the door unless you can see who is on the other side. If you don't know the person and trust him, don't open it. Get your phone ready to dial 911. Even if he looks like a deliveryman or a cop, don't open the door. If he starts trying to break it, call 911 and go hide somewhere, and tell the operator where you are hiding.

Walk with confidence and choose where you are walking, and with whom. Know that drinking and doing drugs and taking chances for the heck of it can put you right in the hands of some psychopath. Risky behavior is stupid behavior, and stupid behavior is going off with some guy you don't really know because your brain is on vacation or you just want to see what happens. Ending up raped and murdered isn't the ending you want. Stay away from risky behavior. Stay smart. Stay as safe as you can.

Eight

●●●●●●●●●●●●●●●●●●●●●●●●●●●●●●●●●●●●●●●

THE **SEX TRADE** AND **SEX TRAFFICKING**

There is a new bogeyman on the block, and it is called sex trafficking. Every time a girl goes missing now, people start saying she might have been taken by sex traffickers. There is now a worldwide search under way for Madeleine McCann, a child who disappeared out of her parent's rental vacation home in Praia da Luz, Portugal, in 2007, when she was three. Her adorable little face is everywhere on the Internet and on posters, and thousands believe that she might have been kidnapped by child pornographers or a sex-trafficking ring and that she is alive and being held captive somewhere in Morocco, Holland, or the Far East.

Little Johnny Gosch, the abducted paperboy whose face was one of the first to be featured by the missing-children-on-milk-cartons campaign more than two decades ago, is believed by many to be alive, including his own mother, who claims that he actually came for a visit one night a few years ago but that he is being controlled by a homosexual sex-trafficking ring that he cannot escape from.

And some still think Natalee Holloway, who vanished in Aruba in 2005, is still alive and being held captive in a sex ring. In spite of Joran van der Sloot's own confession that she died in his arms on the beach (he is presently incarcerated in Peru for the brutal murder of Stephany Flores, another woman who met him in a casino and went off with him), there are people who believe he handed her over to sex traffickers and that she is alive and being forced to prostitute herself somewhere on one of the Caribbean islands.

Yet in reality, all three of these cases have far more probable scenarios. Madeleine McCann either died under unfortunate circumstances in her parents' apartment and they covered up the crime or a local pedophile abducted her and took her back to his house, where he eventually killed her. Johnny Gosch, mostly likely raped and murdered within hours of his disappearance by a child predator, is probably buried on a nearby farm. Natalee Holloway most likely died at the hand of van der Sloot, and he disposed of her body somewhere in the ocean or on the island.

Even women who are known to have been working in the sex trade and believed by the police to have been murdered by their pimps or by serial killers have parents and victims' advocates claiming they have been whisked away by sex traffickers, transported around or out of the country, kept in sexual slavery year after year, hidden away in a nefarious sex ring, never to be free again.

Not How It Happens in the United States and Canada (or in Many Other Countries)

In reality, sex trafficking in the United States and Canada is nowhere near the magnitude it is in places like Thailand, India, and other Far Eastern countries. In fact, what true sex trafficking entails in North America mostly involves foreign women attempting to come to the United States, buying their passage through unscrupulous "businessmen," and finding themselves in houses of prostitution with no passport and a huge bill to pay off to get out of their indentured servitude. It is a crime that increasing numbers of innocent young Asian women (and other wishful immigrants, some from Central America and Mexico and other parts of the world) have been sucked into, and one that authorities are trying to solve. However, it is a fate that befalls only a very few Caucasian, African-American, or legal Hispanic citizens of the United States and Canada.

Yet sex traffickers snatching people off the street has become a hot issue in missing-persons organizations. Why? There are three main reasons this concept has gained traction. First, law enforcement has added the label "sex trafficker" to any pimp who crosses the state line with a prostitute, so that stronger federal laws can be used to apprehend and convict him. So a pimp who drives a girl to a hotel one mile over a state line is now called a sex trafficker. Second, families want more than anything else to believe their missing children (like Elizabeth Smart and Jaycee Dugard, who were not held by sex traffickers but by sexual predators) are alive and may come home one day, and not in a box. Third—and this is the most important point and the reason I am bringing up the sex-trafficking issue—parents do not want to believe their daughters (or sons) could become involved in prostitution through any action of their own, whether that be enticement or coercion, desperation, drugs, or a relationship. Guilt, and denial of their own children's actions, is the reason increasing numbers of people prefer the term "sex trafficking" to "sex trade": it is much easier to believe your child was snatched away than to believe she walked into the situation with some level of cooperation. This fallacy is causing parents to ignore the true dangers out there—the many kinds of prostitution venues that may draw in a naïve girl, the reasons such places can be enticing, how pimps get new girls, and how your own daughter could end up "in the life."

The Truth About How Girls Usually Become Prostitutes

The number one way your daughter will end up in prostitution is through a pimp who will put her on the streets. It is an ugly life; nothing glamorous about it. It is sleazy, seedy, and scummy. Very few girls think, *Wow! Prostituting on the street would be really cool!* Well, there may be a few girls already living in tough neighborhoods and sexually active at a young age who may think it is awesome to get dressed up in garish, sexy outfits and cavort on the corner, making quick bucks, and feeling a level of power and control they lack in their poverty-filled lives. If you live in a struggling neighborhood and your daughter is slipping out at night and seems to thinks some of these street gals are cool, you may want to find out what is going on.

But most girls are going to think that hooking on the street is for crack hoes and is so scary and disgusting, they shudder at the thought. A young girl would never envision this as her future. But one day, she might find herself getting into strangers' cars, turning tricks in alleys, and climbing the steps to the by-the-hour room in a dirty hotel with a man she hopes won't hurt her.

Let's look at how your daughter could end up on the street. It is *not* because a sex trafficker grabbed her on the way from a Girl Scout meeting to the ice cream store. If your straight-A daughter vanishes on the way to babysitting, a serial killer got her, not a sex trafficker. If your daughter ends up on the street, there was an avenue leading her there, and you need to be sure she doesn't start walking in that direction.

Most girls end up as street hookers because they run away from home. As I said, working the stroll is not an enticing career choice, so there has to be no other hope of survival except prostitution. Bus stations are a shopping bazaar for pimps looking for new bodies—those teenage kids who used whatever money they could borrow, earn, or steal for a ride away from home, from the life they thought couldn't get worse. They usually find out it *can* get much worse. Unless a church member or a staffer at a runaway house whisks that child with a target on her forehead away from the clutches of these low-life pimps (and sometimes their female helpers), your child doesn't stand a chance. Your daughter may not even realize the goal of these predators; she may think they want to truly help her find her way in a new city, that they are her friends. Young people tend to turn strangers into friends (in their heads) in a matter of minutes if the strangers appear to be nice or understanding. With no choice but sleeping in a ditch or in a doorway and starving, it is easy for a girl to convince herself that going with this person is the lesser of two evils.

Sometimes, the pimp or one of his women will fake caring for the youngster for a short period of time, gradually acclimatizing the girl to her new situation. Drugs, alcohol, parties, "friendship," affection, clothing, jewelry—whatever helps the child feel temporarily happier and secure, she gets. Bit by bit, she becomes less appalled at the kind of life she sees around her. Then she is introduced to a great way to make money (because at some point she has to contribute to the "home," doesn't she?). By now, she may think this further step down is not such a big deal, or she may have been brainwashed to think prostitution is perfectly fine as an alternative or radical lifestyle (and teens love those antiestablishment and antinormal concepts). She may be scared but feel she has no choice, which, barring running back home or going to a shelter or ending up homeless and hungry, might be true. The door into the life opens, she goes through, and it slams behind her.

Something Is Seriously Wrong If Your Teen Runs Away from Your Home

What can you do to keep your child from running away from home? First of all, her home needs to be a place where she feels safe. She needs to believe staying at home offers her a positive future, even if she thinks that home could be a better place. Abuse, severe neglect, or mental cruelty by parents or by significant others in the home may send her to the Greyhound station one day. If you think your home is an unpleasant place for your daughter, you need to figure out how to change that *before* she takes matters into her own hands. No man, no husband, no woman, no friend, and no personal issues between Mom and Dad should take precedence over your daughter's well-being. Don't say to yourself, "It's not that bad" if it really is that bad. Dealing with the issues now is nothing compared to losing your daughter to prostitution.

Keeping these same problems in the home in mind, be aware that your daughter doesn't have to run away to end up on the streets. It is the most common way, but there are pimps in your neighborhood, near your schools, and at the parties your daughter might sneak out of the house to go to. Emotional problems, a lack of self-confidence, self-hatred, or a sense of hopelessness can make her vulnerable to a slick-talking man who becomes her boyfriend or confidant. Pimps don't pick cheerleaders, prom queens, and top honor-roll students as material for their stable of girls; they spot the unhappy girl in the corner downing straight alcohol, and they know they have a pigeon. By the time you find out your daughter is a "working girl," it may be too late to pull her out. Then she will probably run away again to keep doing what she is doing; after all, she now has a man to "take care of her."

Move Quickly

If you notice your daughter is disappearing at odd times, if you hear she is dating (at age fourteen) an older guy (in his twenties or thirties), if you find overtly sexual comments and photos on her Facebook page, your daughter may be hooking or about to slide into the life. You will have to take strong action because she may no longer care what you think and, in fact, flaunt her life in your face to pay you back for failing in your job as a parent, whether or not you have failed. Call a service in your town or a hotline that helps parents get their girls out of prostitution, and do it before she flees the area.

If your daughter already has run away and is living in some far-away city, you will have to go there, get help to retrieve her (you may need the help of law enforcement), and bring her home, getting her straight into counseling. If your home is not a good place for her to go—after all, it might be the reason she ran off—you will have to take her to a place that specifically helps prostitutes break free of the life.

Pay attention to any signs that your daughter is descending into drug or alcohol abuse; if she develops a chemical dependency, prostitution may be the only way for her to procure more drugs. Her drug dealer may have some associates who can help her earn money. Let's face it, criminals hang around criminals, and if your child is buying from them regularly, she is already in a circle of pretty crappy individuals. Also, trading sex for drugs is the quickest way to the next fix or hit, so one doesn't have to get money for sex to become a prostitute, and every crack whore can tell you how true this is.

I am painting an ugly picture because it is an ugly life. No parent raises her child thinking this would be a fine way for her to live (unless you are one of those parents who forces her own child into prostitution). It is important to accept the fact—yes, the fact—that your child didn't just accidentally get hooked up with a pimp. Her life led her into the pimp's parlor and she got entangled in his web. Even if one out of a thousand times it were true that a sex ring grabbed her, you have the best shot at keeping your daughter safe by keeping her from drifting into an alternative lifestyle, becoming unhappy, hanging around questionable people, and experimenting with drugs and alcohol.

And don't forget this important reality: your daughter may get pulled into prostitution first and then turn to drugs to deal with it. Drugs can lead to prostitution and prostitution can lead to drugs. Furthermore, while sex trafficking doesn't exist in this country in the same manner it does in other countries, where girls are kidnapped and locked in a room to service twenty men a day and moved from secret whorehouse to secret whorehouse in a big sex ring, she *may* end up with a pimp who eventually *does* keep her locked up, and he may move operations to a different location or share her with or sell her to other pimps.

A pimp is like an abusive boyfriend; when you are his, he treats you like property and you lose all say in the matter. So while one could call a certain kind of prostitution sex trafficking, it is important to differentiate it from sex-trafficking rings that kidnap or lure large numbers of children and women into their organizations and, from the very first moment, make them total slaves. Warning women in certain countries to not believe scams that sell them the promise of a rich life somewhere else or warning children, teens, and young women to be very vigilant on the way to the community water pump makes sense, but in the United States, the warning needs to go to parents about the quality of life in the home and their relationship with their child.

Finally, let's put another myth to rest regarding sex trafficking: sex traffickers don't need to kidnap white girls and blondes and bring the wrath of law enforcement down upon their heads. Why? Because there is no shortage of willing white girls and blondes who will go into prostitution without much objection. All you have to do to prove this is go on the Internet and see just how many attractive white and blond girls are in porn films. Now, it is true that some of these girls are trapped in the porn life, but they didn't get abducted into it. They thought it was going to be fun or a great way to get to Hollywood, or they wanted the money. Some are exhibitionists and like people watching them have sex. It is easier to lure girls or have their creepy parents bring them to you. Stealing them is unnecessary and a bad business practice.

I *do* want to warn you parents of one exception to this rule and tell you how it works. Be aware of scams labeled "Club in Tokyo Seeking Blond Hostesses" that your daughter might run across in the newspaper or on Craigslist. This *is* one way that girls end up as prostitutes in Asian countries. The offer is for a free trip and housing and a chance to see Japan (or whatever country) and work in an "upscale" club patronized by rich businessmen. It sounds pretty good. I answered an ad just like that when I lived in Hollywood years ago, when I was nineteen. Luckily for me, I thought it sounded dangerous and I didn't get on the plane; otherwise, I might have spent a life hooking for the Yakuza, the Japanese mafia, and that would not have been too great.

Fancy Names for Prostitution Services: Don't Be Fooled

Okay, some of you are now feeling pretty comfortable that *your* daughter is not going to end up on the street. If your home life isn't too bad, you are probably right. But you still have to worry about your daughter becoming a prostitute, just not at the lowest rung of the profession. Do you know what businesses are fronts for prostitution? Does your daughter? Here is a list of "services" and occupations that are nothing but fancy names for prostitution or gateways to prostitution.

Massage parlors
Escort services
Bottle girls
Private photography sessions

Tantric erotic massages

Dance-hall girls

Go-go girls

Lap dancers

Strippers

Modeling services

"Adult services" found on Craigslist, in Yellow Page ads, and in newspapers

Erotic or porn films

I am sure I will be getting hate mail from women who insist that *they* are not hookers, even though they are in the businesses I just listed, and that they do not exchange sex for money in their work. Okay, there may be *some* (go-go girls and strippers who perform but do not prostitute themselves; and there will be erotic or porn film actresses who argue it is not prostitution but art that just happens to involved sex and a paycheck). However, *all* the other services are hands-down prostitution services.

Here is how it works. A young woman sees an ad offering lots of money for giving massages in a massage "studio" that (it turns out) has waterbeds instead of massage tables. She goes for an interview and is told she will have to give the massage topless, or perhaps dressed in a skimpy outfit, and she is expected to give the customer a massage of the erogenous zone, aka a "hand job" after she completes a Swedish fingertip massage, which involves slathering the man with oil and running her fingertips over him. For this, she may make something like thirty-five dollars or fifty dollars, depending on the time frame and the fanciness of the room. Already, the girl is thinking, *Oh my God, I can make fifty dollars in an hour just for, um, well, jacking a guy off? Yuck, but okay, I will give it a try.* This is already prostitution, but she won't get arrested for it because the money paid for the massage is only for a massage, even if it is well understood by both masseuse and client that a hand job is included. The police can't arrest her because no discussion of money for sex occurs.

Now, one thinks, this just a mild form of prostitution, but at least the girl isn't really having sex with the man. Think again. Most men do not come in for a hand job, unless they are cheapskates. They want more. They want intercourse or a blow job or anal sex or something even kinkier. If the girl refuses to ever do anything more than masturbate the customers, a whole lot of complaints will be coming in to the manager of the massage parlor, and she will be fired. She learns this quickly, and these are her two choices: quit or become a prostitute for real. A good percentage of girls stay.

"Not *my* daughter!" you say. Okay, you admit, it is true, she has had a couple of boyfriends before she reached age eighteen and she has been on the Pill for the last four years, but she comes from a decent enough family and is going to community college.

Well, unless she is a church girl, has extremely strict morals, or has her eye on becoming a politician, she may find the lure of so much money intoxicating in spite of what she has to do to get it. She could work a regular job for $10 an hour or she could make $100 to $150 an hour doing something she has already given away for free. And if the sex wasn't all that great, anyway, getting paid for it rather than giving it away may not seem that bad a deal.

She is on the fence on the first night she works at the parlor. Her customer is very pleasant—not all that hideous—and they chat. He asks if she will do more. She hems and haws, and he lays five $20 bills on the table. She is already half naked and he is naked, and for only a few quick minutes of sex, the extra $100 is hers. She tells herself that she is just testing the waters and will probably not do it again. After the customer leaves, she pockets the money. The next man comes in and, what the heck—she has already crossed the line, and the thrill of doubling her money is intoxicating. She does it a few more times that night. Then she goes home and sits on her bed and tosses her stack of $20 bills in the air, whooping and laughing. She normally would have to work for weeks full-time to earn the same amount of money (and no taxes are taken out of her illegal bounty). She is back at the parlor the next night, and at the end of the week she goes on a shopping spree and buys whatever she feels like. She takes friends out, buys them drinks, pays for their dinners, and feels rich and powerful; she has found one heck of an "easy" way to make great money. After a while, she may not really want to continue doing what she is doing, but it is now far too difficult to take a crappy job again making minimum wage, so if she wants to keep her lifestyle, she finds herself stuck in the life.

She also starts finding that college is a bit boring and she can no longer relate to "non-working girls," so she drops out of school and stops hanging around her regular friends. From that point on, she is on a merry-go-round of making and spending money, possibly sliding into drugs and alcohol as a method of coping with the degradation she feels but tries to ignore, along with the fact that the career she has chosen has no future. She may realize that finding a nice boyfriend or husband is going to be more difficult now, and her attitude toward men is getting worse by the day. Having children presents a problem—prostitution doesn't offer maternity leave—and the thought of having a child while hooking is a bit uncomfortable.

If she finds the strength, because after all she does have a decent background and education, she may one day pull herself out of the life and tough it out as a regular person again. But a lot of damage may have been done to her physically or psychologically. Just because a form of prostitution may not require a pimp—and massage parlors, escort services, and bottle-girl work does not—it doesn't mean the hooking doesn't have its dangers and lasting negative effects.

Escort-service work tends to pay even more than massage

parlors if the service sends the girl to a high-priced hotel. Well-heeled businessmen may pay hundreds for an hour or two with a girl or a thousand for the night. Don't let your daughter believe (or tell you) that escort work is simply providing companionship for a lonely out-of-towner with dinner or a movie. She may show up the first night thinking that is the case and refuse to do more, but she will soon be fired if she does not end the evening in the manner the gentlemen expects. If a girl works as an escort for more than a couple of nights, I can guarantee you, she is a hooker.

Dance-hall work almost seems like an old-fashioned job. Like an Arthur Murray studio party night, fellows show up and buy tickets for slow dances with the ladies. Each time they pick a girl from the row, they hand her a ticket and she tucks it in a rubber band she has around her finger. There is nothing particularly untoward going on in the dance hall. She dances and chats with her partners, and everything is perfectly pleasant. If she is a good dancer, attractive, and attentive, she will get more dances and make more money. She may actually think when she takes on the work and whirls her way around the floor that this is quite a nice job! Not much different than teaching ballroom dance; she just doesn't have to be as skilled as a professional dancer, and everyone has an enjoyable evening.

But this is not what the job is about. The purpose of the place is to provide an opportunity for men to find a girl to go home with, or at least go *someplace* with (like the parking lot). Like the other fronts for prostitution, the boss is going to pull the girl aside after a few nights and ask her why she is frustrating the customers. What does she think these men come here for? Just to glide around the floor with a woman? She will realize then that she either starts doing her job the right way or she doesn't need to show up again.

I speak from experience. I answered that employment ad while living in Hollywood, and I got a huge stack of tickets under my rubber band the first night on the job—and got fired that very same night for leaving alone.

Strippers and go-go girls have a job they are paid to do, and in theory, this is all that is required. Some clubs actually hold to that standard, but believe me, most club owners look the other way when a girl leaves with a different guy every night. There is money to be made in the after-hours work, and the lure of quick cash, for a woman already half naked (or completely naked), is hard to turn down. Also, some club owners get surly if a girl is too goody-two-shoes and will swiftly replace her with someone more "free-spirited."

Being a bottle girl in New York City, Las Vegas, or Miami is the Cadillac of prostitution. These girls dine with the bigwigs and sports superstars. They are usually very beautiful and well-dressed and appear to be just partying with the guys, or maybe they appear to be their girlfriends. In reality, a price comes with the girls, and these rich men toss money around quite freely; a girl in this high end of the business can live quite a lavish life. She receives cash, expensive jewelry, condos, and cars. She doesn't have to service men like a factory-line worker, and she appears to those outside the business to be more of a man's mistress or a date. Her family and friends may think she is working as a bar girl, a model, or an actress. They may just think that she has a rich man in her life. Being a steady mistress to a high roller or having even a one-night stand with a handsome rich man doesn't seem so much like prostitution as the other forms do, but the rules are basically the same; sex is clearly part of the deal. These men are not spending big bucks to just see some pretty faces at the table. Again, no pimp is necessary and there are no sleazy motel rooms or violence, but it is still what it is. Your daughter doesn't need to waste her life being a paid courtesan.

Finally, tell your daughter that doing porn films is one of the worst ways to wreck her life. Some young girls really believe that "acting" in these movies will eventually bring them a real role in a Hollywood movie. I can't say that this has never happened, but she might as well play the lottery as believe this; her odds will be about the same, and she won't destroy herself in the process. Porn movies pay horribly, for the most part, and often require unprotected sex with dozens of men, sometimes dozens in just one movie. Anal sex is a common theme these days, so the increased risk of HIV comes along with these acts and can cause rectal prolapse and damage to the anus. The sex is often quite brutal: violent pounding and introduction of large objects or more than one penis at a time into the vagina or anus, causing unnatural stretching of the orifices. Sadistic sex with bondage, spanking, whipping, and other forms of torture is not that rare. Your daughter could end up suffering massive pain and degradation. Often porn workers take massive amounts of drugs to withstand the pain of the sex acts and to deal with the humiliation. The stories women tell about their lives in the world of porn are extremely upsetting. Don't let your daughter go there.

One of the worst aspects of porn is something girls often don't think about. Once upon a time, the magazine she ended up in naked, or the videotape that includes her sex act, might have been seen by only a few people. If she got lucky, she could quit the business and no coworker or future husband (or son or daughter) would ever see it. Now, with the Internet, whatever she does will stay in cyberspace forever. Many a beauty queen or actress has experienced this, even Dr. Laura (Laura Schlessinger), the former radio psychologist, who posed for some nude photos for a boyfriend years ago. The pictures have proliferated across hundreds of websites. Forever is a long time to have your reputation attacked and for the humiliation to continue. At least a prostitute might be able to quit the life and put it behind her and have her past be her past. But the Internet will never let sleeping dogs lie. Those pictures and videos will always be there.

Make Sure She Knows the Score

I am sure by now you are pretty repulsed by the many opportunities there are for your daughter to end up as a "working girl." You may wonder (even if you don't think it can happen to your daughter, that she is too smart or too moral) what to say to her about this. My advice is to be perfectly frank. If she is old enough to actually choose to sell herself for sex, get lured into it by the money, or be cajoled into it by a man she thinks is her friend or lover, she is old enough to hear what is out there in the world. She needs to know why she should avoid prostitution and porn like the plague.

Talk to her about the two basic kinds of prostitution, the ugly kind on the street and the kind that has pretty frosting disguising it (especially the high-end work). Make sure you discuss what drugs can do to your mind and your pride and how they can quickly make you do things you never thought you would do. Talk to her about the kind of men who hang around the fast life, how no decent man takes a girl he cares about into that degrading world. Make sure she knows that running away from home or even going unprepared to another city can quickly put her in a desperate situation and that no guy who pops up to help her is likely to be doing it without an evil motive attached. Make sure she knows she can come to you and find a way to solve her problems without turning to strangers or questionable friends.

Be sure she understands that the glitter of places like Las Vegas and New York may be seductive but that the allure comes with a price that may destroy her life. If she finds the concept of modeling and acting and the fast life in general exciting, help her understand what can really happen if she pursues these things. Encourage her to do her research through knowledgeable people—not a girlfriend who tells her what fun she will have—and find alternatives in honorable careers and safe venues. There *are* modeling and acting jobs that are legitimate, of course, but young girls often don't know the difference between those and prostitution fronts, and they may find out too late that they have chosen the wrong ones. And in case you think times have changed, the casting couch is still a reality in much of the modeling and acting world; having sex with producers and photographers is often the price one pays to get opportunities, most of which never materialize. Teach your daughter to respect herself enough to not go down these roads. Help her plan her future and teach her the art of being patient in achieving success (long-term goals instead of instant gratification). If she sees a bright future in an interesting profession, she will not find these other "careers" very inviting.

Dear Daughter,

I know life isn't perfect here at home, although we try our best to be a good family. If you ever think you can't stand living here anymore, please come talk to me and together we will see how we can make things better. Most important, don't run away! Girls who run away end up in even worse situations, picked up by pimps at the Greyhound station, turned out onto the streets to be prostitutes, beaten and abused and given drugs. Most of these girls die by age thirty-four from disease or murder or suicide.

If you are depressed or bored, please stay away from drugs, especially the scary kind. You know what I mean—crack, cocaine, meth, GHB, heroin, OxyContin, ice, speed. That is the kind of stuff that will get you addicted and force you to have to find a way, like selling yourself for sex, to get money for more drugs. Come talk to me and let's see if we can find you a way to make life fun without messing up your head.

And finally, watch out for that girl with the great hair extensions, tats, and designer clothing who tells you that you can make big money "just" by going on a date with a businessman, by giving some guy a massage, or by hanging out at a restaurant with some superstars. She is leaving out the fact that you have to have sex with all of them in order to get that money. Anytime you give sex for money, and that includes "acting" in porn films, you are a hooker, and who wants to grow up to be a hooker? I think you can do many more wonderful things in life than spend it giving men a cheap thrill, don't you?

Final Thoughts

· ·

*E*very *day it seems we hear* of another new story of a girl who has been horribly victimized. No doubt parents can't help but think, *Thank God that wasn't* my *daughter.* Then they worry that next time it will be. I am sure that worry is what propelled you to buy this book and learn as much as you can about keeping your daughter from becoming a victim. I hope I have armed you with the information you need.

The "Dear Daughter" letters can be used at any time you think they would be useful. You can also rewrite the letters in your own words and add anything you particularly think your daughter needs to know. You can also have your daughter read excerpts of the book that you feel comfortable having her read. If she is about to graduate from high school or is in college, you can hand her the book and tell her you got it to learn about ways to help her stay safe but that you think she is mature enough to read the book and see what information Pat Brown was sharing with the adults in her life.

Please go over the various safety issues with your daughter, not all at the same time, perhaps, but one at a time. You can offer small pieces of advice at appropriate times; for example, "Let's not walk on that side of the road with the bushes; let's stay on this side on the sidewalk with the houses so we can be safer" or "When you leave work at night, don't have anyone you don't know walk you to your car, including that security guard you know nothing about." Spend much longer periods going over the serious issues brought up in each chapter and help your daughter understand their importance and how they apply to her, and together develop safe plans and practices to help her make good decisions and stay safe.

If you now know a lot more than you did before you read *How to Save Your Daughter's Life*—more about psychopaths, predators, and the dangerous situations your daughter might find herself in—then my mission has been accomplished! I wish your daughter the best of luck on her road into adulthood, and to you; you obviously love her very much. May her journey be a safe one.

Hugs,
Criminal Profiler Pat Brown

About the Author

● ●

*P**at Brown** is a nationally known criminal profiler, television commentator, author, and founder and CEO of the Sexual Homicide Exchange (SHE) and the Pat Brown Criminal Profiling Agency. She has provided crime commentary and profiling and forensic analysis in more than 2,000 television and radio appearances in the United States and across the globe. She can be seen regularly on news programs on CNN, MSNBC, and FOX and is a frequent guest of *The Today Show, the CBS Early Show, Inside Edition,* HLN's *Prime News, Issues with Jane Velez-Mitchell, and Dr. Drew.*

For four seasons, Brown profiled crimes on the weekly Court TV crime show *I, Detective.* She is the host of the 2004 Discovery Channel documentary *The Mysterious Death of Cleopatra.* In the spring of 2006, Brown went inside one of Florida's maximum-security prisons to interview a child murderer for the Discovery Channel show *Evil Minds.* In 2010 she profiled a new Jack the Ripper suspect for Investigation Discovery's

Mystery Files. Brown is the authof of *Only the Truth; The Profiler: My Life Hunting Serial Killers and Psychopaths*; and *Killing for Sport: Inside the Minds of Serial Killers*; and *The Murder of Cleopatra.* She contributed special feature content included in the fifteenth anniversary edition, 2006 DVD release of Quentin Tarantino's crime classic *Reservoir Dogs* and in the 2003 *Profiler: Season Two* home DVD.

Brown holds a master's degree in Criminal Justice from Boston University and developed the first criminal profiling certificate program in the country for Excelsior College. To learn more about Pat Brown's profiling work, law enforcement training, and community education, visit www. CriminalProfilerPatBrown.com.

Index

abortion, 45, 145
Adderall, 57
ADHD, 57
advertising, 17
alcohol, 41, 49–52
    and sex, 50
    drunk driving, 51
amphetamines (*see also* drugs), 57–58
An Education, 143
anal sex, 69, 239–240
anger, 14–15, 158
Anthony, Casey, 66, 113
antidepressants, 57–58
antisocial behavior, 14–15
Astley, Lauren, 162–163

barbituates (*see also* drugs), 69
bath salts (*see also* drugs), 56
Bennet, Anna Elizabeth, 29
Berkowitz, David, 194
bodyguards, 183–184
books, 16
    Baby-Sitters Club, 28
    Harry Potter, 29–30
    inappropriate, 27–29
    Twilight books, 29, 30–34
Boston Strangler, 196
boyfriends

and family relationships, 154–155
breaking up with, 177–179,
        181–183
criteria, 152–153, 159–160
dangerous boyfriends, 156–158
parental involvement, 151–153
setting a good example, 153–154
stalkers, 171–173, 177–178
why girls pick bad ones, 160–161
Brandes, Bernd, 102
bullying
    online (*see also* Internet), 103–104
    perspective, 115–118
    preventing, 104–105, 110–114
Bundy, Ted, 194–195
Bustamante, Alyssa, 24

Cannibal Café, 101–102
cell phones and smart phones, 126–127
chat rooms (*see* Internet)
Clark, Raymond J., 176
cocaine (*see also* drugs), 54
    crack, 55

date rape
    alcohol, 65, 77–78, 84–85
    date rape drug, 50
    false reporting, 79–80

date rape (cont'd from page 249)
    investigating, 70–71, 73–74, 77–78,
      80–81
    preventing, 82–86
    prosecution, 66–68
    saying no, 78–79
    without alcohol, 81–82
Dateline, To Catch a Predator, 94–95
dating, 13
    rules, 163–164
de Becker, Gavin, 216
"Dear Daughter" letter
    boyfriends and relationships, 166–
      168
    entertainment, 37
    date rape and rape, 87–88
    drugs and gangs, 63
    Internet, 127–128
    prostitution, 243
    serial predators, 218–219
    stalkers, 190–191
depression, 14–15, 57
discipline, 3–5
    behavior, 4–6
    corporal, 4, 7
drugs, 48–49
    and parental use, 57
    gateway drugs, 53
    strength, 52
Dugard, Jaycee, 136

Ecstasy (*see also* drugs), 55
empathy, 157–158
erotomania, 175, 185
Eye for an Eye, 26

Facebook, 89, 98, 101, 103
    and gangs, 60
    bullying, 108–112
    controlling, 121, 126

prostitution, 229
stalking, 173, 178
family
    dangerous relationships, 130–131,
      141–142
    dating criminals, 137–140
    in prison, 140
    significant others, 133–137
Field, Sally, 26
Flores, Stephany, 152, 222
freedom
    cultural, 40–41
    earning, 11–12
Fritzl, Josef, 130
Fujita, Nathaniel, 162

gangs, 47, 58–61
    uncovering, 60–61
Garrido, Phillip, 136
GHP (*see also* drugs), 55–56
Girl Scouts, 12
Gosch, Johnny, 222
goth culture, 35–36, 106–107
Green River Killer, 195
Grim Sleeper, 196

Hansen, Chris, 94–95
Harry Potter books, 29–30
HIV, 44, 63, 146, 239–240
hobbies, 26–27
Holloway, Natalee, 152, 222
home protection, 212–214
homeschooling, 12
hooking up, 44
huffing (*see also* drugs), 56

Internet, 16, 89
    bullying, 103–104, 108–110
    bullying, stopping, 110–115,
      119–123

chat rooms, 94–97, 123–125
   gaming, 100–101
   pornography, 91–92, 240
   safety, 90, 126–127
   sexual predators, 94–100
   sick sites, 101–102

Jeffs, Warren, 153

kissing, 43

Lady Gaga, 22
Le, Annie, 176–177
Lemmon, Aliahna, 141–142
Little Witch, 29
Long Island Serial Killer, 196
lying, 158, 163–164

Malvo, Lee Boyd, 194
manipulation, 158
marijuana (*see also* drugs), 52–53
   potency, 52
marriage
   and sex, 35
   forced, 40
McCann, Madeleine, 221–222
Meiwes, Armin, 102
methamphetamines (*see also* drugs),
   54–55
Meyer, Stephenie (*see also* Twilight),
   150
movies, 17–18
   horror movies, 25–26
   sexualization, 24–25
Muhammed, John Allen, 194
music
   limiting, 22–23
MySpace, 89
nutmeg (*see also* drugs), 56

older men, 142–148, 151

Pacino, Al, 116
parenting (*see also* discipline)
   delaying behaviors, 10–12
   healthy home environment, 15–16
   isolation, 130–133
   making excuses, 7–8
   negativity, 14–15, 24–25
parking lots, 210–211
parties, 13
peer pressure, 47
personality disorders, 132, 156, 165,
   178–180
   signs of, 157–159
   stalkers, 171–172, 174
Planned Parenthood, 41, 45
pornography (*see also* Internet), 69
   accessibility, 90–92
   damage to actresses, 239–240
   negative influence, 92–94
pregnancy, 44–46
prostitution, 224, 234–236
   and drugs, 230, 236
   bottle girls, 238–239
   dance halls, 237–238
   escort services, 236–237
   kinds of businesses, 232–234
   massage parlors, 234–236
   preventing, 228–229, 241–242
   recruiting girls, 225–228
   strippers, 238
psychopaths (*see* personality disorders)
punishment (*see* discipline)

rap, 22
rape (*see also* date rape)
   cultural attitudes, 75–77
   example, 71–73
   in marriage, 40

rape (*see also* date rape)
    rape kit, 207
    serial rape, 195–196, 198, 200–201
restraining orders (*see also* stalker),
    186
Ritalin, 57
runaways, 227
    preventing, 227–228

Scarface, 116
Schlessinger, Laura, 240
self-esteem, 148–149
self-defense, 200–202
    and cars, 207–208
    good methods, 203–205
    once captured, 208
    safety tips, 209–210
serial killers, 158
    as security guards, 211–212
    disguised, 212–213
    frequency, 194–195
    high-risk behavior, 214–216
    methods of attack, 204–207
sexting, 103
Sexual Homicide Exchange, 90
sex (*see also* date rape)
    differentiating from rape, 69–70
    exploration, 10–11, 14–15
    sexual sadism, 207
sex trafficking, 230–231
    Asian "club hostess" scams,
        231–232
    methods of trafficking women,
        223–224
    prevalence, 224
    race of victims, 231
sexual predators, 94–100
school, 42–43
    sex education, 44
    unhealthy environments, 46,
        106–107

social media (*see* Facebook *and*
    Internet)
Son of Sam, 194
speed (*see also* drugs), 54, 57
Spencer, Timothy, 214
sports, teams
    coaches, 9–10
stalkers
    and murder, 170
    bodyguards, 183–184
    boyfriends, 171–173, 177–178
    dealing with, 184–185, 187–188
    causes of, 170–171
    increasing incidence, 169–170
    preventing, 179–182
    restraining orders, 186
    techniques of stalking, 173
    wannabe boyfriends, 174–176
Stockholm Syndrome, 97–98
Stine, R. L. 28
suicide, 34, 124
Sutherland, Kiefer, 26

television, 16, 19–20
    limiting, 20–22
Triangle of Victimization, 197–198
Twilight, 29, 30–34, 148–151
Twitter, 89, 103, 109–110, 121–122

van der Sloot, Joran, 152, 222
video games, 16, 24
videos (*see* music)

Woods, Tiger, 151

young childhood, 1
    behavioral problems, 3–4
    parenting, 1–3, 6–7

Zodiac Killer, 194